SANTORINI

TRAVEL GUIDE

2024-2025

Everything you need for this Island Adventure: Tips, Highlights and More

Mark Martin

Copyright © 2024 **Mark Martin**

Santorini

Welcome to Santorini

Map of Santorini

Just make sure you get QR code scanner on your phone, scan it, open the website and view the map.

Table of Contents

Introduction

The Allure of Santorini

Santorini stands out as a jewel in the Aegean Sea, a place where nature's raw power and human ingenuity have combined to create a destination unlike any other. This crescent-shaped island, born from volcanic fury, now beckons travelers with its striking landscapes and rich cultural tapestry.

A Glimpse into Santorini's Past

The story of Santorini begins long before recorded history. Around 3600 years ago, a massive volcanic eruption shook the very foundations of the ancient world. This cataclysmic event, one of the largest in Earth's history, forever altered the island's landscape. The eruption left behind a flooded caldera, steep cliffs, and a legacy that continues to shape Santorini's identity.

Before the eruption, Santorini was home to the Minoans, an advanced civilization that thrived during the Bronze Age. Their settlement at Akrotiri, buried and preserved by volcanic ash, offers a window into a sophisticated society that existed over three millennia ago. The discovery of Akrotiri in the 20th century revealed frescoes, pottery, and urban planning that rivaled other ancient cultures of its time.

Following the Minoan era, Santorini saw a parade of civilizations leave their mark. The Phoenicians, Dorians, Romans, Byzantines, Venetians, and Ottomans all contributed to the island's rich cultural mosaic. Each group left behind architectural, culinary, and cultural influences that blend seamlessly with the island's Greek heritage.

The Geological Marvel

Santorini's geology is a testament to the Earth's dynamic nature. The island's distinctive crescent shape cradles a massive caldera, a remnant of the ancient volcano that continues to shape the island's destiny. This unique formation creates a natural amphitheater, with white-washed villages perched precariously on the caldera's edge, offering breathtaking views of the Aegean.

The volcanic activity blessed Santorini with fertile soil, ideal for cultivation. The island's vineyards, some of the oldest in the world, produce distinctive wines from grapes grown in the mineral-rich earth. The same volcanic forces created Santorini's famous beaches, where visitors can find sands in shades of red, black, and white – each telling a different chapter of the island's geological story.

A Canvas of Colors

Santorini's visual appeal goes beyond its natural wonders. The island is a study in contrasts, where the deep blue of the Aegean meets the stark white of the iconic Cycladic architecture. This color palette, complemented by the warm hues of sunset and the dark volcanic rocks, creates a setting that has inspired artists and photographers for generations.

The villages of Santorini, with their maze-like streets and blue-domed churches, offer a picturesque scene at every turn. Oia, perched on the northern tip of the island, is world-renowned for its sunset views. As the day ends, the village becomes a gathering point for visitors and locals alike, all drawn by the spectacle of the sun sinking into the sea, painting the sky in a riot of colors.

A Culinary Journey

Santorini's unique environment has given rise to a distinctive culinary tradition. The island's cuisine is a reflection of its history, climate, and volcanic terroir. Local specialties like fava (a puree made from yellow split peas), tomatokeftedes (tomato fritters), and white eggplant showcase the flavors born from Santorini's volcanic soil.

The island's wines deserve special mention. The indigenous Assyrtiko grape thrives in Santorini's harsh conditions, producing crisp, mineral-rich wines that perfectly complement the local seafood. Many wineries offer tours and tastings, allowing visitors to sample these unique vintages while learning about the island's ancient viticultural practices.

Villages and Vistas

Santorini's villages each offer a unique perspective on island life. Fira, the bustling capital, combines traditional architecture with modern amenities. Its winding streets are lined with shops, restaurants, and galleries, making it a hub of activity day and night.

Imerovigli, known as the (balcony to the Aegean) offers some of the most stunning views on the island. This quiet village is perfect for those seeking a more relaxed atmosphere while still enjoying proximity to Santorini's attractions.

For a glimpse into Santorini's past, the village of Pyrgos offers a well-preserved example of medieval architecture. Its hillside location provides panoramic views of the island, while its narrow streets and traditional houses transport visitors to another era.

Beaches: A Volcanic Legacy

Santorini's beaches are as diverse as they are beautiful. The famous Red Beach, with its rust-colored cliffs and sand, offers a striking backdrop for sunbathers and swimmers. The long stretches of black sand at Perissa and Kamari beaches provide ample space for relaxation and water sports.

For those seeking seclusion, the White Beach, accessible only by boat, offers a tranquil escape. Here, white cliffs contrast sharply with the deep blue waters, creating a secluded paradise.

Cultural Riches

Santorini's cultural offerings are as rich as its natural beauty. The Museum of Prehistoric Thera in Fira houses artifacts from the excavations at Akrotiri, offering insights into the island's ancient past. For those interested in the island's more recent history, the Maritime Museum in Oia chronicles Santorini's long relationship with the sea.

Throughout the year, Santorini comes alive with festivals and events that celebrate its cultural heritage. From religious feasts to wine festivals, these events offer visitors a chance to engage with local traditions and experience the warmth of Greek hospitality.

Adventure and Exploration

While Santorini is known for its romantic atmosphere and stunning views, it also offers plenty of opportunities for adventure. Hiking trails crisscross the island, with the path from Fira to Oia being particularly popular. This trail offers unparalleled views of the caldera and passes through picturesque villages along the way.

For those looking to explore beyond the island's shores, boat tours offer a unique perspective on Santorini's volcanic landscape. Many tours include stops at the nearby volcanic islands of Nea Kameni and Palea Kameni, where visitors can hike to the crater of an active volcano and swim in natural hot springs.

Preserving Paradise

As Santorini's popularity has grown, so too has the awareness of the need to preserve its unique environment and culture. Efforts are underway to promote sustainable tourism practices, ensuring that future generations can continue to enjoy the island's beauty.

Visitors are encouraged to respect local customs, support eco-friendly initiatives, and be mindful of their impact on the island. By choosing locally-owned businesses, participating in beach clean-ups, and respecting protected areas, travelers can play a part in preserving Santorini's natural and cultural heritage.

Planning Your Visit

Santorini welcomes visitors year-round, though the experience can vary greatly depending on the season. The summer months of June through August see the largest crowds and highest prices, but also offer the fullest range of activities and services.

For those seeking a quieter experience, the shoulder seasons of spring and fall offer milder weather and fewer crowds. Winter visits, while limited in terms of open businesses, provide a unique opportunity to see a different side of the island, when local life takes center stage.

Regardless of when you choose to visit, Santorini offers a wealth of accommodations to suit every budget and preference. From luxury cave houses carved into the caldera cliffs to family-run guesthouses in traditional villages, the island caters to all types of travelers.

A Journey of Discovery

Santorini is more than just a destination; it's an experience that engages all the senses. The island's beauty lies not just in its famous sunsets and white-washed buildings, but in the stories etched into its landscape, the flavors of its cuisine, and the warmth of its people.

Santorini offers a journey of discovery. Each visit reveals new facets of this multifaceted island, inviting travelers to create their own unique connection with this extraordinary place.

As you plan your journey to Santorini, keep in mind that the true magic of the island often lies in the unexpected moments – a chance encounter with a local artisan, a hidden viewpoint discovered during a morning walk, or the perfect taverna found down a winding alley. Allow yourself the freedom to wander, to get lost in the beauty of the moment, and to create memories that will last a lifetime.

Santorini stands as a testament to the enduring allure of the Greek islands. It's a place where myth and reality intertwine, where ancient history and modern luxury coexist in harmony. As you turn the pages of this guide, you'll find the tools and insights needed to craft your own Santorini adventure. Whether it's your first visit or a return to a beloved destination, Santorini is ready to captivate you with its timeless charm.

Chapter 1

Planning Your Trip

Getting ready for your Santorini adventure requires careful consideration of various factors. This chapter will guide you through the essential aspects of planning your trip, ensuring you make the most of your time on this enchanting Greek island.

Best Times to Visit

Santorini's climate and tourist seasons play a crucial role in determining the best time for your visit. Each season offers a unique experience:

Summer (June to August)

The peak tourist season brings warm temperatures, ranging from 70°F to 85°F (21°C to 29°C). The island buzzes with activity, and all attractions, restaurants, and shops are open. However, this period also sees the highest prices and largest crowds.

Benefits:

- Perfect weather for beach activities

- Lively atmosphere with numerous events and festivals

- All tourist facilities fully operational

Limitations:

- Crowded attractions and beaches

- Higher prices for accommodations and activities

- Potential for occasional heatwaves

Spring (April to May) and Fall (September to October)

These shoulder seasons offer a pleasant balance of good weather and fewer crowds. Temperatures typically range from 60°F to 75°F (15°C to 24°C).

Benefits:

- Mild weather ideal for sightseeing and outdoor activities

- Lower prices compared to summer

- Less crowded attractions

Limitations:

- Some tourist facilities might have limited hours

- Sea temperatures may be cooler for swimming

Winter (November to March)

The off-season in Santorini sees cooler temperatures, ranging from 50°F to 60°F (10°C to 15°C), and occasional rainfall. Many tourist facilities close or operate with reduced hours.

Benefits:

- Lowest prices for accommodations

- Authentic local atmosphere

- Ideal for photography without crowds

Limitations:

- Many restaurants and attractions closed or with limited hours

- Cooler temperatures and potential for rainy days

- Reduced ferry and flight schedules

Getting There

By Air

Santorini International Airport (JTR) serves as the main gateway for air travelers. During peak season, direct flights are available from many European cities. Year-round, you can reach Santorini via connecting flights through Athens.

<u>Tips for flying to Santorini:</u>

- Book flights well in advance, especially for summer travel

- Consider flexible dates to find better deals

- Check baggage allowances, as some budget airlines have strict policies

By Sea

Ferries connect Santorini to other Greek islands and the mainland. The main port, Athinios, handles most ferry traffic, while the Old Port in Fira receives cruise ships.

Ferry options include:

High-speed catamarans: Faster but more expensive

Conventional ferries: Slower but more economical

Tips for ferry travel:

- Book tickets in advance during peak season

- Check the ferry schedule, as it varies by season

- Be prepared for potential delays due to weather conditions

Visa Requirements

Greece is part of the Schengen Area, and visa requirements depend on your nationality:

- **EU citizens:** No visa required for stays of any length

- US, Canadian, Australian, and many other nationalities: No visa required for stays up to 90 days within a 180-day period

- **Other nationalities:** Check with the Greek embassy or consulate in your country

Always ensure your passport is valid for at least six months beyond your planned stay.

Transportation on the Island

Santorini offers various transportation options to suit different preferences and budgets:

Rental Cars and ATVs

Renting a vehicle gives you the freedom to explore the island at your own pace. Many agencies offer cars and ATVs (quad bikes) for rent.

Benefits:

- Flexibility to visit remote areas

- Convenience for families or groups

Limitations:

- Limited parking in popular areas

- Narrow, winding roads can be challenging for inexperienced drivers

Tips:

- Book in advance during peak season

- Ensure you have an International Driving Permit if required

- Check insurance coverage carefully

Public Buses

The local bus network connects major towns and attractions. It's an economical option, but services can be less frequent outside peak season.

Benefits:

- Affordable

- Covers most popular destinations

Limitations:

- Can be crowded during peak times

- Limited schedule, especially in off-season

Tips:

- Check the latest bus schedule upon arrival

- Have exact change ready for ticket purchases

Taxis

Taxis are available but can be scarce during busy periods. They're a good option for short trips or airport transfers.

Benefits:

- Convenient for direct trips

- Air-conditioned comfort

Limitations:

- More expensive than public transport

- May be hard to find during peak times

Tips:

- Agree on the fare before starting the journey

- Book in advance for airport transfers

Water Taxis

Water taxis connect some beaches and ports, offering a scenic transportation alternative.

Benefits:

- Unique way to see the coastline

- Avoids road traffic

Limitations:

- Limited routes

- Weather-dependent

Accommodations

Santorini offers a wide range of accommodations to suit various preferences and budgets:

Luxury Hotels and Resorts

Many high-end options are located along the caldera edge, offering stunning views.

Benefits:

- Exceptional service and amenities

- Often include infinity pools and spa facilities

Limitations:

- High prices, especially in peak season

- Can be booked out months in advance

Boutique Hotels

These smaller, often family-run hotels provide a more personalized experience.

Vacation Rentals

Apartments, villas, and traditional cave houses are available for rent.

Benefits:

- More space and privacy

- Option to self-cater

Budget Options

Hostels and budget hotels are available, particularly in Fira and Perissa.

Benefits:

- More affordable

Tips for booking accommodations:

- Reserve well in advance for peak season stays

- Consider location carefully – caldera views come at a premium

- Read recent reviews from multiple sources

- Check cancellation policies, especially if traveling in shoulder seasons

Budgeting

Santorini can be expensive, especially during peak season. Here's a rough guide to help you budget:

Accommodation

- Budget: €30-70 per night

- Mid-range: €70-200 per night

- Luxury: €200+ per night

Meals

- Budget: €10-20 per person per meal

- Mid-range: €20-40 per person per meal

- High-end: €40+ per person per meal

Activities

- Museum entries: €3-10

- Boat tours: €30-100

- Wine tastings: €15-50

Tips for saving money:

- Travel during shoulder season for better rates

- Consider accommodations in less touristy areas

- Take advantage of free activities like hiking and beach-going

- Look for hotels that include breakfast

Packing Essentials

What to bring depends on the season, but here are some essentials:

- Comfortable walking shoes for uneven terrain

- Sunscreen, sunglasses, and a hat (summer)

- Light layers for evening cool (spring/fall)

- Waterproof jacket (winter)

- Swimwear and beach towel

- Adapter for European outlets

- Portable charger for your devices

Health and Safety

Santorini is generally a safe destination, but it's wise to take standard precautions:

- Purchase travel insurance that covers medical emergencies

- Bring any necessary prescription medications

- Use sun protection and stay hydrated, especially in summer

- Be cautious when swimming in unfamiliar areas

- Keep valuables secure, particularly in crowded tourist areas

Healthcare on the island:

- The main hospital is located in Fira

- Pharmacies are widely available in towns

- For EU citizens, the European Health Insurance Card (EHIC) provides access to state-provided healthcare

Cultural Considerations

- Dress modestly when visiting churches

- Ask permission before photographing locals

- Learn a few basic Greek phrases – locals appreciate the effort

- Tip in restaurants (10-15% is standard) unless a service charge is included

Tech and Connectivity

Staying connected in Santorini:

- Wi-Fi is widely available in hotels, cafes, and restaurants

- Consider purchasing a local SIM card for data access

- Download offline maps and translation apps before your trip

Day Trip and Island-Hopping Options

Consider exploring beyond Santorini:

- Visit nearby Thirassia for a glimpse of traditional island life

- Take a day trip to Ios or Naxos

- Join a multi-day cruise to explore more of the Cyclades

When planning these excursions:

- Check ferry schedules, which can vary by season

- Book tickets in advance during peak periods

- Allow ample time for transfers and potential delays

Special Considerations

Accessibility

Santorini's terrain can be challenging for those with mobility issues. Many hotels and restaurants have steps, and some beaches are difficult to access. Research accessible accommodations and tours if needed.

Family Travel

If traveling with children:

- Choose family-friendly accommodations with appropriate amenities

- Plan activities suitable for kids, like beach days and boat tours

- Be cautious with young children near cliff edges in caldera towns

Solo Travel

Santorini is generally safe for solo travelers. Consider:

- Staying in social accommodations like hostels to meet other travelers

- Joining group tours for activities

- Taking standard safety precautions, especially at night

Pre-Trip Checklist

As your trip approaches:

- Confirm all bookings (flights, accommodations, tours)

- Inform your bank of your travel plans

- Make copies of important documents

- Check the latest travel advisories

Chapter 2

Where to Stay

Accommodations for Every Budget

Luxury Cliffside Hotels

These accommodations often feature infinity pools, spa services, and gourmet restaurants.

Locations

Luxury hotels are primarily found in:

- Oia

- Imerovigli

- Firostefani

- Fira

What to Expect

- Breathtaking caldera views

- Private balconies or terraces

- High-end amenities (spa services, infinity pools)

- Personalized service

- Gourmet dining options

Oia Hotel

Price Range

Expect to pay upwards of €300 per night, with some suites costing over €1000 during peak season.

Benefits:

- Unparalleled views

- Top-notch service and amenities

- Romantic atmosphere

Limitation:

- High prices

- Can be crowded during peak season

- Often booked months in advance

Tips

- Book well in advance, especially for summer stays

- Check for package deals that include meals or spa treatments

- Consider staying during shoulder season for better rates

Boutique Hotels

Boutique hotels offer a more intimate setting with personalized service. They often feature unique designs that blend traditional Cycladic architecture with modern amenities.

Locations

Found throughout the island, including:

- Fira

- Firostefani

- Pyrgos

- Megalochori

What to Expect

- Individually designed rooms

- Personalized service

- Local character and charm

- Smaller property with fewer rooms

Price Range

Prices typically range from €150 to €500 per night, depending on location and season.

Tips

- Read reviews to understand each property's unique offerings

- Contact the hotel directly for personalized recommendations or services

- Look for boutique hotels in less touristy villages for a more authentic experience

Budget-Friendly Options

Santorini offers various budget-friendly accommodations for travelers looking to save on lodging.

Types of Budget Accommodations

1. Hostels

2. Guesthouses

3. Budget hotels

4. Camping sites (limited options)

Locations

Budget options are more common in:

- Perissa

- Kamari

- Fira (outskirts)

- Karterados

What to Expect

- Basic amenities

- Shared facilities in hostels

- Simple, clean rooms

- Often family-run in the case of guesthouses

Price Range

Prices can range from €20 for a hostel bed to €100 for a basic hotel room, depending on the season.

Tips

- Book in advance for summer stays, as budget options fill up quickly

- Consider staying in beach towns like Perissa for more affordable options

- Look for places that offer free breakfast to save on meal costs

Vacation Rentals

Vacation rentals, including apartments, villas, and traditional cave houses, offer a home-away-from-home experience.

Types of Vacation Rentals

1. Apartments

2. Villas

3. Traditional cave houses

4. Windmills (unique option)

Locations

Available throughout the island, including:

- Oia

- Fira

- Akrotiri

- Emporio

What to Expect

- More space compared to hotel rooms

- Kitchen facilities for self-catering

- Privacy

- Local neighborhood experience

Price Range

Prices vary widely, from €50 for a small apartment to over €1000 for a luxury villa with a pool.

Benefits:

- Cost-effective for families or groups

- Ability to cook meals and save on dining out

- Local living experience

Tips

- Read reviews carefully and check for verified photos

- Communicate with the host about check-in procedures and local tips

- Consider the location carefully, as some rentals may be in residential areas far from attractions

Unique Accommodations

Santorini offers several unique lodging options for those looking for an extraordinary stay.

Types of Unique Accommodations

1. Cave houses

2. Windmill conversions

3. Eco-lodges

4. Boat stays

Locations

Scattered across the island, with concentrations in:

- Oia (cave houses)

- Emporio (windmills)

- Rural areas (eco-lodges)

What to Expect

- Distinctive architectural features

- Unusual layouts or designs

- Potential for limited modern amenities in some cases

- One-of-a-kind experience

Price Range

Prices vary greatly, from €100 for a simple cave house to over €500 for a luxury windmill conversion.

Benefits:

- Memorable, Instagram-worthy stays

- Cultural or historical significance

- Bragging rights

Tips

- Book well in advance as these properties are often in high demand

- Check for any physical requirements (e.g., lots of stairs in cave houses)

- Ask about modern amenities if they're important to you

Choosing the Right Location

Your choice of location can significantly impact your Santorini experience. Here's a breakdown of the main areas:

Oia

- **Known for:** Stunning sunsets, luxury hotels, romantic atmosphere

- **Best for:** Couples, luxury travelers, photographers

Limitation: Crowded during peak times, expensive

Fira

Known for: Nightlife, shopping, central location

Best for: Young travelers, those who want to be in the middle of the action

Imerovigli

- **Known for:** Quiet atmosphere, excellent views, upscale hotels

- **Best for**: Couples seeking tranquility, luxury travelers

Firostefani

Known for: Caldera views, proximity to Fira, quieter atmosphere

Best for: Those who want to be near Fira but in a more relaxed setting

Kamari and Perissa

- **Known for:** Black sand beaches, more affordable accommodations

- **Best for:** Beach lovers, budget travelers, families

Pyrgos

Known for: Traditional village atmosphere, panoramic views

Best for: Travelers seeking authenticity, wine enthusiasts

Factors to Consider When Booking

When choosing your accommodation in Santorini, consider the following factors:

1. View: Caldera views come at a premium. Decide if it's worth the extra cost.

2. Accessibility: Many hotels have numerous stairs. If mobility is an issue, inquire about elevator access.

3. Pool: A pool can be a great relief from the heat. Not all hotels have them, so check if this is important to you.

4. Air conditioning: Essential for summer visits. Confirm that your room has it.

5. Noise levels: If you're a light sleeper, avoid staying in the center of Fira.

6. Transportation: Consider proximity to bus routes if you're not renting a vehicle.

7. Parking: If you're renting a car, check if the

accommodation offers parking.

8. Wi-Fi: While most places offer Wi-Fi, speeds can vary. If you need reliable internet, inquire about connection quality.

9. Breakfast: Many hotels offer breakfast. This can be a great way to save money and start your day conveniently.

10. Cancellation policy: Given Santorini's seasonal nature, it's wise to choose bookings with flexible cancellation policies.

Booking Tips

To ensure you get the best accommodation for your needs and budget, follow these tips:

1. Book early: The best places fill up quickly, especially for summer stays.

2. Compare prices: Use multiple booking sites and compare with the hotel's direct rates.

3. Read recent reviews: Pay attention to recent guest experiences, especially regarding cleanliness and service.

4. Look for package deals: Some hotels offer packages that include transfers, meals, or activities.

5. Consider shoulder season: You can often find great deals with good weather in May-June or September-October.

6. Communicate directly: Reaching out to the property directly can sometimes result in better rates or room assignments.

7. Check the map: Ensure you understand the exact location of the property in relation to attractions and amenities.

8. Understand the fees: Be aware of any additional fees for things like airport transfers or city taxes.

9. Loyalty programs: If you're a member of any hotel loyalty programs, check if they have partner properties in Santorini.

10. Local stays: Consider family-run guesthouses for a more authentic experience and often better value.

Seasonal Considerations

Your accommodation options and prices will vary depending on when you visit Santorini:

High Season (June to August)

- Highest prices

- All accommodations open

- Need to book months in advance

- Full range of services available

Shoulder Season (April-May, September-October)

- More moderate prices

- Most accommodations open

- Pleasant weather

- Good balance of availability and services

Low Season (November to March)

- Lowest prices

- Many accommodations closed

- Limited services

- Quieter atmosphere, good for budget travelers

Special Accommodations

Family-Friendly Options

- Look for hotels with family rooms or suites

- Consider vacation rentals for more space

- Check for kid-friendly amenities like children's pools or play areas

- Kamari and Perissa are often good choices for families

Accessible Accommodations

- Limited options due to Santorini's terrain

- Look for newer hotels which may have better accessibility

- Always contact the property directly to discuss specific needs

- Consider staying in flatter areas like Kamari

Eco-Friendly Stays

- Look for properties with sustainable practices

- Some hotels use solar power or have water conservation programs

- Consider traditional cave houses which are naturally energy-efficient

Making the Most of Your Stay

No matter where you choose to stay in Santorini, here are some tips to enhance your accommodation experience:

1. Engage with staff: Local staff can provide invaluable tips and recommendations.

2. Enjoy your balcony or terrace: Many rooms come with outdoor space – make use of it!

3. Try the local breakfast: If your hotel offers breakfast, it's a great way to try local specialties.

4. Use hotel services: Many hotels offer services like tour bookings or restaurant reservations, often at no extra cost.

5. Respect the property: Many buildings in Santorini are old or traditionally constructed. Be mindful and treat the space with care.

6. Be a good neighbor: Especially in vacation rentals, be considerate of local residents.

7. Leave reviews: Help future travelers by leaving honest, constructive reviews of your stay.

Chapter 3

Exploring Santorini's Picturesque Villages

Each village has its own unique character, offering visitors a glimpse into the island's rich history and culture.

Oia: Sunset Paradise and Iconic Blue Domes

Oia, pronounced **Ia**, is perhaps the most famous village in Santorini, known for its stunning sunsets and iconic blue-domed churches.

Location and Character

Situated on the northern tip of the island, Oia clings to the cliff face of the caldera. Its whitewashed buildings, blue-domed churches, and winding pathways create a postcard-perfect scene.

Things to See and Do

1. Sunset Viewing: Find a spot along the castle ruins for the famous Oia sunset.

2. Blue Domes: Photograph the iconic blue-domed churches.

3. Ammoudi Bay: Visit this small port below Oia for fresh seafood and swimming.

4. Art Galleries: Browse local and international art in the village's many galleries.

5. Atlantis Books: Visit this charming, cave-like bookstore.

Best Times to Visit

- Early morning for photography and peaceful walks

- Late afternoon for the sunset (arrive early to secure a good spot)

- Avoid midday in summer when cruise ship crowds are at their peak

Dining Recommendations

- Melitini for traditional Greek meze

- Lauda for high-end dining with a view

- PitoGyros for quick, delicious gyros

Shopping

- Gold Street for jewelry

- Oia-C for designer clothing

- Atlantis Books for literature and local authors

Tips

- Wear comfortable shoes for the uneven cobblestone streets

- Book restaurants in advance, especially for sunset times

- Be prepared for crowds, particularly during sunset hours

Fira: The Bustling Capital

Fira, the capital of Santorini, offers a mix of traditional charm and modern amenities, making it a hub of activity on the island.

Location and Character

Perched on the caldera cliff, Fira is centrally located and serves as the main transportation hub. It combines traditional Cycladic architecture with a more cosmopolitan vibe.

Things to See and Do

1. Cable Car Ride: Take the cable car from the old port for panoramic views

2. Museum of Prehistoric Thera: Explore artifacts from the island's ancient history

3. Orthodox Metropolitan Cathedral: Visit this impressive church in the town center

4. Nightlife: Dance the night away in Fira's many clubs and bars

5. Caldera Walk: Hike the scenic path to Oia (allow 2-3 hours)

Best Times to Visit

- Mornings for shopping and sightseeing

- Evenings for dining and nightlife

- Avoid midday during summer when cruise passengers crowd the streets

Dining Recommendations

- Argo for seafood with a view

- Lucky's Souvlakis for quick, tasty gyros

- Ouzeri for traditional Greek cuisine

Shopping

- Fira's main street for souvenirs and local products

- Gold factories for jewelry

- Drakkar for leather goods

Tips

- Use the central bus station to explore other parts of the island

- Visit the old port via cable car, donkey ride, or on foot (be prepared for stairs)

- Book accommodations away from the main street if you're a light sleeper

Imerovigli: The Balcony to the Aegean

Known as the (balcony to the Aegean,) Imerovigli offers some of the most spectacular views on the island in a quieter setting than Oia or Fira.

Location and Character

Situated at the highest point of the caldera cliff, Imerovigli is a peaceful village with luxurious hotels and romantic atmosphere.

Things to See and Do

1. Skaros Rock: Hike to this former fortress for incredible views

2. Anastasi Church: Visit this picturesque blue-domed church

3. Hiking: Walk the scenic path to Fira or Oia

4. Sunset Watching: Enjoy quieter sunset views than in Oia

- Any time of day for peaceful walks and photography

- Evening for romantic dinners with a view

Dining Recommendations

- La Maison for fine dining with a view

- Anogi for traditional Greek cuisine

- The Athenian House for upscale Greek fusion

Shopping

Limited shopping options, but a few boutiques and local craft shops are available.

Tips

- Book accommodations well in advance, especially for caldera view hotels

- Prepare for a quieter atmosphere with fewer amenities than Fira or Oia

- Rent a car or use taxis, as bus service is limited

Pyrgos: A Step Back in Time

Pyrgos offers a glimpse into traditional Santorinian life, away from the tourist crowds of the caldera villages.

Location and Character

Located inland, Pyrgos is the highest village on the island. Its well-preserved kasteli (castle) and traditional architecture make it a hidden gem.

Things to See and Do

1. Kasteli: Explore the medieval castle ruins

2. Profitis Ilias Monastery: Visit this 18th-century monastery for panoramic views

3. Wine Tasting: Visit nearby wineries for Santorini's famous wines

4. Easter Celebrations: Watch the village light up with candles on Good Friday

Best Times to Visit

- Morning for clear views from the village's high points

- Evening for a quieter dinner experience

- During Easter for traditional celebrations

Dining Recommendations

- Cava Alta for Mediterranean cuisine with a view

- Kantouni for traditional taverna experience

- Selene for high-end, locally-sourced Greek cuisine

Shopping

- Local art galleries for unique souvenirs

- Traditional products shops for Santorinian specialties

Tips

- Rent a car or take a taxi, as bus service is limited

- Wear comfortable shoes for exploring the steep, narrow streets

- Visit during the off-season for a truly authentic experience

Megalochori: Quaint and Traditional

Megalochori is a picturesque village known for its traditional architecture and connection to Santorini's wine industry.

Location and Character

Located in the southwest of the island, Megalochori is surrounded by vineyards and features neoclassical mansions and traditional cave houses.

Things to See and Do

1. Bell Towers: Admire the village's distinctive bell towers

2. Wine Tours: Visit nearby wineries like Gavalas and Venetsanos

3. Symposion Cultural Center: Learn about Greek mythology and music

4. Heart of Santorini: Find this unique heart-shaped hole in the caldera

Best Times to Visit

- Morning for peaceful village walks

- Afternoon for wine tasting tours

- Evening for quiet dinners in the village square

Dining Recommendations

- Feggera for creative Greek cuisine

- Raki for traditional meze

- Taverna Geromanolis for home-style Greek food

Shopping

- Local shops for traditional products and wine

- Art galleries for unique pieces

Tips

- Consider staying in Megalochori for a quieter, more authentic experience

- Combine a visit with wine tasting at nearby wineries

- Explore the village on foot to discover hidden gems

Emporio: Fortress Village with Medieval Charm

Emporio, the largest village on Santorini, offers a unique blend of medieval architecture and traditional island life.

Location and Character

Located in the south of the island, Emporio is known for its well-preserved kasteli (castle) and maze-like streets.

Things to See and Do

1. Kasteli: Explore the medieval castle and its surrounding neighborhood

2. Goulas (Tower): Visit this Venetian tower in the village center

3. Windmills: See the eight traditional windmills on the village outskirts

4. Churches: Admire the numerous blue-domed churches scattered throughout

Best Times to Visit

- Morning for exploring the castle area

- Midday for lunch in local tavernas

- Avoid early afternoon in summer when many shops close for siesta

Dining Recommendations

- Afoí Koutsogianopoúloi for authentic Greek cuisine

- To Kafenedaki tou Emboriou for coffee and light meals

- Metaxi Mas for creative Greek dishes

Shopping

- Local shops for traditional products

- Small boutiques for unique clothing and accessories

Tips

- Wear comfortable shoes for walking on cobblestone streets

- Visit early in the day to avoid afternoon heat

- Combine with a trip to nearby Perissa beach

Akrotiri: Ancient History and Red Beach

While not a typical village, Akrotiri is a must-visit for its archaeological site and nearby Red Beach.

Location and Character

Located on the southern tip of the island, Akrotiri is famous for its prehistoric settlement and striking red cliffs.

Things to See and Do

1. Akrotiri Archaeological Site: Explore this well-preserved Minoan city

2. Red Beach: Visit this unique beach with red cliffs and sand

3. Lighthouse: See one of the oldest lighthouses in Greece

4. La Ponta Venetian Tower: Attend music performances in this restored tower

Best Times to Visit

- Early morning to beat the crowds at the archaeological site

- Late afternoon for visiting Red Beach

- Avoid midday in summer due to intense heat

Dining Recommendations

- The Cave of Nikolas for fresh seafood

- Melina's Tavern for traditional Greek cuisine

- Akrotiri Fish Tavern for seaside dining

Shopping

- Souvenir shops near the archaeological site

- Local products at small markets

Tips

- Combine a visit to the archaeological site with a trip to Red Beach

- Bring water and sun protection, especially in summer

- Book a guided tour for the archaeological site for better understanding

Karterados: Off the Beaten Path

Karterados offers a glimpse into local Santorinian life, away from the tourist crowds.

Location and Character

Located just outside Fira, Karterados is a traditional village with cave houses and a laid-back atmosphere.

Things to See and Do

1. Cave Houses: Admire the traditional cave houses built into the cliff

2. Agios Nikolaos Church: Visit this charming blue-domed church

3. Local Life: Experience authentic Greek village life

4. Walks: Enjoy peaceful walks through the village streets

Best Times to Visit

- Any time of day for a quiet village experience

- Evening for dining with locals

Dining Recommendations

- Katerados for home-style Greek cuisine

- Elia Restaurant for traditional dishes with a modern twist

- To Pinakio for meze and ouzo

Shopping

Limited shopping options, mostly small local stores for essentials.

Tips

- Consider staying here for a more budget-friendly, authentic experience

- Use as a base to explore other parts of the island

- Rent a car or scooter for easy access to other villages

Firostefani: Caldera Views Without the Crowds

Firostefani offers stunning caldera views similar to Fira but with a more relaxed atmosphere.

Location and Character

Located just north of Fira, Firostefani is quieter but still offers easy access to the capital's amenities.

Things to See and Do

1. Agios Nikolaos Monastery: Visit this picturesque monastery

2. Caldera Views: Enjoy panoramic views without Fira's crowds

3. Hiking: Walk the scenic path to Imerovigli or Fira

4. Sunset Watching: Find a quiet spot for beautiful sunsets

Best Times to Visit

- Morning for peaceful walks and photography

- Evening for romantic dinners with a view

Dining Recommendations

- Aktaion for traditional Greek cuisine

- Vanilia for cocktails with a view

- Remvi for upscale dining

Shopping

Limited shopping options, but close to Fira for more variety.

Tips

- Book accommodations with caldera views for the best experience

- Enjoy the proximity to Fira without staying in the busy center

- Be prepared for some steep paths and stairs

Village Hopping in Santorini

Exploring Santorini's villages is one of the best ways to experience the island's true character. Each village offers something unique:

- Oia for iconic sunsets and blue domes

- Fira for shopping and nightlife

- Imerovigli for luxury and tranquility

- Pyrgos for traditional charm

- Megalochori for wine and quietude

- Emporio for medieval architecture

- Akrotiri for ancient history

- Karterados for local life

- Firostefani for caldera views without crowds

<u>To make the most of your village exploration:</u>

1. Plan your visits around the best times for each village

2. Use a mix of transportation: walking, buses, and maybe a rental car

3. Try local cuisine in each village for a diverse culinary experience

4. Interact with locals for insider tips and authentic experiences

5. Respect local customs and the quiet nature of some villages

6. Carry a camera – each village offers unique photo opportunities

7. Be prepared for lots of walking and stairs

8. Stay hydrated and use sun protection, especially in summer

Chapter 4

Beaches and Coastal Adventures

Red Beach: A Geological Wonder

Red Beach is one of Santorini's most famous and visually striking coastal areas, known for its dramatic red cliffs and unique landscape.

Location and Access

- Situated near the ancient site of Akrotiri in the southern part of the island

- Accessible by a short hike from the parking area (about 10 minutes)

- Alternative access by boat from Akrotiri port

Beach Characteristics

- Small, pebbly beach with red and black volcanic stones

- Red cliffs provide a stunning backdrop

- Clear, deep blue waters ideal for swimming and snorkeling

Activities

- Swimming and sunbathing

- Snorkeling along the base of the cliffs

- Photography (especially during golden hour)

Facilities

- Limited facilities (no permanent structures due to landslide risk)

- Occasional beach umbrellas and chairs for rent (seasonal)

- No lifeguards on duty

Best Times to Visit

- Early morning or late afternoon to avoid midday heat

- Shoulder season (May-June or September-October) for fewer crowds

Safety Considerations

- Be cautious of potential falling rocks from the cliffs

- Wear sturdy shoes for the short hike to the beach

- Check current conditions, as the beach is occasionally closed due to landslide risks

Nearby Attractions

- Akrotiri Archaeological Site

- Akrotiri Lighthouse

- White Beach (accessible by boat from Red Beach)

Black Beach (Perissa): Volcanic Sands and Water Sports

Perissa Beach, also known as Black Beach, is one of Santorini's most popular and well-developed beach areas, known for its long stretch of black sand and numerous facilities.

Location and Access

- Located on the southeastern coast of Santorini

- Easily accessible by bus from Fira or by car

- Ample parking available near the beach

Beach Characteristics

- Long stretch of fine black sand

- Clear, shallow waters perfect for swimming

- Backed by numerous restaurants, bars, and hotels

Activities

- Swimming and sunbathing

- Water sports (jet skiing, parasailing, paddleboarding)

- Beach volleyball

- Diving (PADI-certified diving center available)

Facilities

- Numerous sunbeds and umbrellas for rent

- Showers and changing rooms

- Lifeguards on duty during peak season

- Beach bars and restaurants

  - ### Best Times to Visit

- Early morning for a quiet swim

- Midday for full beach atmosphere and activities

- Evening for beachfront dining and nightlife

Unique Features

- Mesa Vouno mountain provides a dramatic backdrop

- Connection to Perivolos Beach, forming a 7km stretch of black sand

Nearby Attractions

- Ancient Thera (accessible via a steep path from the beach)

- Perissa village for dining and accommodation

- Water park (great for families)

Tips

- The black sand can get very hot in summer - bring appropriate footwear

- Visit in the shoulder season for a more relaxed atmosphere

- Try local seafood at one of the beachfront tavernas

White Beach: Secluded Beauty

White Beach, while less famous than its red and black counterparts, offers a unique and secluded beach experience.

Location and Access

- Located near Akrotiri, south of Red Beach

- Accessible only by boat from Akrotiri port or Red Beach

- Some boat tours from other parts of the island include stops here

Beach Characteristics

- Small, pebbly beach surrounded by white cliffs

- Clear, deep waters ideal for swimming and snorkeling

- Limited space, providing an intimate beach experience

Activities

- Swimming and snorkeling

- Sunbathing

- Cave exploring (small caves in the cliffs)

Facilities

- Very limited facilities due to its secluded nature

- Occasional beach umbrellas (bring your own to be safe)

- No lifeguards on duty

Best Times to Visit

- Morning for the calmest waters

- Midday for the best lighting for photos

- Avoid windy days as the beach can become uncomfortable

Unique Features

- White pumice cliffs create a striking contrast with the blue sea

- One of the least crowded beaches on Santorini

Tips

- Bring water, snacks, and sun protection as there are no facilities

- Wear water shoes to navigate the pebbly shore comfortably

- Consider combining a visit with Red Beach for a diverse beach day

Kamari Beach: Family-Friendly Resort Area

Kamari Beach offers a perfect blend of natural beauty and modern amenities, making it ideal for families and those seeking comfort alongside their beach experience.

Location and Access

- Located on the eastern coast of Santorini

- Easily accessible by bus from Fira or by car

- Close to Santorini Airport

Beach Characteristics

- Long stretch of dark grey sand and pebbles

- Clear waters with a gradual depth increase

- Backed by a promenade filled with shops, restaurants, and hotels

Activities

- Swimming and sunbathing

- Water sports (including windsurfing and paddleboarding)

- Open-air cinema near the beach

- Diving (multiple diving centers available)

Facilities

- Numerous sunbeds and umbrellas for rent

- Showers and changing rooms

- Lifeguards on duty during peak season

- Wide range of restaurants, cafes, and bars

Best Times to Visit

- Morning for a peaceful swim

- Afternoon for full beach atmosphere

- Evening for dining and nightlife along the promenade

Unique Features

- Mesa Vouno mountain provides a dramatic backdrop

- Paved beachfront promenade perfect for evening strolls

Nearby Attractions

- Ancient Thera (accessible via a hiking trail or by car)

- Wine Museum

- Kamari village for shopping and dining

Tips

- The beach can get crowded in peak season - arrive early to secure a spot

- Try the local wineries in the nearby hills

- Visit the open-air cinema for a unique evening experience

Vlychada Beach: Lunar Landscape and Marina

Vlychada Beach offers a unique landscape with its sculpted pumice cliffs, creating an almost otherworldly beach experience.

Location and Access

- Located on the southern coast of Santorini

- Accessible by car or local bus (less frequent than to other beaches)

- Parking available near the beach and marina

Beach Characteristics

- Long beach with a mix of black sand and pebbles
- Striking white cliffs sculpted by wind and sea
- Usually less crowded than other popular beaches

Activities

- Swimming and sunbathing
- Wind and kite surfing (popular due to frequent winds)
- Exploring the marina and fishing port
- Hiking along the cliffs

Facilities

- Some sunbeds and umbrellas for rent (less developed than Perissa or Kamari)

- A few tavernas and cafes near the beach and marina

- No lifeguards on duty

Best Times to Visit

- Morning for calm waters and fewer people

- Late afternoon for stunning sunset views

- Windy afternoons for wind and kite surfing

Unique Features

- Sculpted cliffs resembling a lunar landscape

- Working fishing port and marina adding local color

Nearby Attractions

- Tomato Industrial Museum

- Monastery of Profitis Ilias (for panoramic views)

- Megalochori village (for traditional architecture and wineries)

Tips

- Bring sun protection as shade is limited

- Be prepared for wind, especially in the afternoon

- Combine your beach visit with a seafood meal at the marina

Beach Hopping by Boat

One of the best ways to experience Santorini's diverse coastline is by boat. Many operators offer day trips that allow you to visit multiple beaches and swim in secluded coves.

Popular Boat Tour Routes

1. Caldera Tour: Visit the volcano, hot springs, and Thirassia island

2. South Coast Tour: Stop at Red Beach, White Beach, and Black Beach

3. Sunset Cruise: Sail along the coast and watch the famous Santorini sunset

What to Expect on a Boat Tour

- Multiple swimming and snorkeling stops

- Views of the caldera and coastal cliffs from the sea

- Often includes lunch or dinner onboard

- Commentary on Santorini's geology and history

Types of Boats Available

- Large catamarans for stable, comfortable cruising

- Traditional wooden boats for an authentic experience

- Luxury yachts for private, high-end tours

- Speed boats for thrill-seekers

Best Times for Boat Tours

- Morning departures for calmer seas

- Afternoon departures for sunset views

- Shoulder season for fewer crowds and pleasant temperatures

Tips for Boat Tours

- Book in advance, especially in high season

- Bring sun protection, swimwear, and a towel

- Choose a tour that matches your interests (relaxation, adventure, photography)

- Consider a small group or private tour for a more personalized experience

Coastal Hiking: Trails with a View

Santorini's coastline offers some spectacular hiking opportunities, combining exercise with breathtaking views.

Popular Coastal Hikes

1. Fira to Oia: A classic 10km hike along the caldera's edge

2. Perissa to Ancient Thera: Steep climb with rewarding views

3. Akrotiri Lighthouse Trail: Easy coastal walk with sunset views

What to Expect on Coastal Hikes

- Uneven terrain and steps in many areas

- Exposure to sun and wind

- Breathtaking views of the Aegean and surrounding islands

- Opportunities to pass through picturesque villages

Best Times for Hiking

- Early morning or late afternoon to avoid midday heat

- Spring or fall for comfortable temperatures and wildflowers

Safety Tips for Coastal Hiking

- Wear sturdy, closed-toe shoes

- Bring plenty of water and sun protection

- Inform someone of your hiking plans

- Stay on marked trails and away from cliff edges

Water Sports and Activities

Santorini's beaches and coastal areas offer a variety of water sports and activities for all levels of adventurers.

Popular Water Sports

1. Snorkeling and Diving

- Best spots: Caldera sites, Nea Kameni, Palea Kameni

- PADI-certified dive centers in Perissa and Kamari

- Visibility typically excellent due to clear waters

2. Kayaking and Stand-Up Paddleboarding

- Rentals available at many beaches

- Guided tours around the caldera available

3. Jet Skiing and Parasailing

- Available at Perivolos and Perissa beaches

- Age and experience restrictions may apply

4. Windsurfing and Kitesurfing

- Best spots: Perissa and Monolithos beaches

- Equipment rental and lessons available

- Best conditions typically in the afternoon when winds pick up

Fishing Trips

- Half-day and full-day fishing excursions available

- Departures from various ports around the island

- Opportunity to catch and cook your own dinner

Sailing Lessons

- Several sailing schools offer short courses

- Learn the basics of sailing in the Aegean

- Multi-day courses available for more in-depth instruction

Coastal Wildlife and Marine Life

While Santorini's waters may not be as diverse as some other Mediterranean locations, there's still plenty of marine life to observe.

Marine Life You Might Encounter

- Various species of fish (groupers, parrotfish, damselfish)

- Octopuses and squid

- Sea urchins and starfish

- Occasional sea turtles (loggerhead turtles)

Best Spots for Marine Life Observation

- Underwater caves near Akrotiri

- Rocky areas around Nea Kameni

- Perissa and Kamari reef areas

Responsible Wildlife Viewing

- Do not touch or remove marine life

- Use reef-safe sunscreen to protect the marine ecosystem

- Participate in local beach clean-up initiatives

Beach Safety and Etiquette

Enjoying Santorini's beaches responsibly ensures a safe and pleasant experience for all visitors.

Safety Tips

- Swim in designated areas and respect flag warnings

- Be cautious of strong currents, especially near the caldera

- Use sun protection and stay hydrated

- Be aware of sea urchins in rocky areas

Beach Etiquette

- Respect local customs regarding appropriate beachwear

- Use designated changing areas rather than changing on the beach

- Do not remove sand, pebbles, or other natural materials as souvenirs

- Dispose of trash properly and consider participating in beach clean-ups

Accessibility Information

- Kamari and Perissa beaches have some accessible facilities

- Some boat tours offer accessibility options - inquire when booking

Coastal Dining: Seaside Tavernas and Beach Bars

Must-Try Coastal Dishes

- Grilled octopus

- Santorinian fava

- Fresh fish (ask for the catch of the day)

- Greek salad with local tomatoes and capers

Notable Beach Restaurants

- Dimitris Taverna (Ammoudi Bay): Fresh seafood with a view

- The 41 (Kamari): Upscale dining on the beachfront

- Tranquilo (Perissa): Relaxed atmosphere with vegetarian options

- Dolphins Fish Taverna (Vlychada): Traditional taverna by the marina

Beach Bar Culture

- Many beaches have beach bars offering cocktails and snacks

- Some organize beach parties and events, especially in high season

- Jojo Beach Bar (Perivolos) and Wet Stories (Perissa) are popular spots

Chapter 5

Culinary Delights: Tasting Santorini

Santorini's cuisine is a vibrant tapestry of flavors, woven from the island's volcanic soil, sun-kissed produce, and centuries-old traditions. As you embark on your gastronomic journey through this Aegean paradise, prepare your taste buds for an explosion of authentic Greek tastes that will linger in your memory long after you've left the island's shores.

Local Specialties: A Symphony of Flavors

Fava: The Golden Treasure of Santorini

- Santorini's fava is not your ordinary legume. This creamy, yellow split-pea puree is the island's culinary claim to fame. Unlike fava beans found elsewhere, Santorini's variety is smaller, sweeter, and more tender, thanks to the mineral-rich volcanic soil.

- Picture yourself in a cozy taverna, the salty sea breeze ruffling your hair as you dip a chunk of crusty bread into a bowl of velvety fava. The earthy, nutty flavor is often enhanced with a drizzle of fruity olive oil, a sprinkle of chopped onions, and a squeeze of lemon. It's simple yet profoundly satisfying – a true taste of Santorini on your plate.

- For the best fava experience, head to the village of Oia. There, you'll find family-run restaurants where grandmothers still lovingly prepare this dish using recipes passed down through generations. Don't be shy – ask the locals about their favorite way to enjoy fava. You might discover some secret family twists that'll make your taste buds dance!

Tomatokeftedes: Crispy Bites of Sunshine

- If there's one dish that captures the essence of Santorini's sun-soaked fields, it's tomatokeftedes. These crispy tomato fritters are a beloved meze (appetizer) that you'll find yourself craving long after your holiday ends.

- Made with the island's famous cherry tomatoes – small, intensely flavored fruits that thrive in the arid climate – tomatokeftedes are a testament to Santorinian ingenuity. Mixed with onions, mint, and sometimes a touch of feta, these fritters are lightly fried to golden perfection.

- As you bite into a tomatokeftede, notice how the crisp exterior gives way to a soft, juicy center bursting with concentrated tomato flavor. It's like tasting Santorini's sunshine in one delightful morsel. Pair them with a chilled glass of Assyrtiko wine, and you've got yourself a match made in culinary heaven.

- For an authentic tomatokeftedes experience, venture into the lesser-known village of Megalochori. Here, away from the tourist crowds, you will find hole-in-the-wall eateries where the recipe hasn't changed in decades. Strike up a conversation with the owner – they might just share their secret ingredient with you!

White Eggplant: The Unsung Hero of Santorinian Cuisine

- When you think of eggplant, you probably picture the deep purple variety. But Santorini's white eggplant is a game-changer. Smaller, sweeter, and less bitter than its purple cousin, this local cultivar is a true delicacy.

- Often grilled and served as part of a meze platter, white eggplant has a delicate flavor that pairs beautifully with other local ingredients. You might find it stuffed with tomatoes and feta, or pureed into a silky dip reminiscent of baba ganoush.

- For a truly unique experience, seek out a restaurant that serves white eggplant ice cream. Yes, you read that right! This unusual dessert is a testament to the versatility of Santorini's produce and the creativity of its chefs. The subtle, sweet flavor of the eggplant is transformed into a creamy, refreshing treat that's perfect for those hot Grecian afternoons.

Wine Tasting and Vineyard Tours: Sipping Santorini's Liquid Gold

Assyrtiko: The Star of Santorinian Wines

- No culinary journey through Santorini would be complete without diving into its world-renowned wine scene. At the heart of this viticulture tradition is Assyrtiko, a white grape variety that thrives in Santorini's harsh, volcanic environment.

- As you sip a glass of Assyrtiko, close your eyes and let the flavors transport you. The wine's high acidity and mineral notes are a direct result of the volcanic terroir, creating a unique taste profile that wine enthusiasts often describe as "liquid rocks." You'll detect hints of citrus, perhaps a whisper of herbs, all underscored by a distinct salinity that speaks of the surrounding Aegean Sea.

- To truly appreciate Assyrtiko, book a tasting at one of Santorini's many wineries. Estate Argyros, founded in 1903, offers an excellent introduction to the island's winemaking heritage. As you stand in their sun-drenched vineyards, notice the unique "kouloura" system – vines trained into low, circular baskets to protect the grapes from harsh winds and maximize exposure to morning dew, crucial in this arid climate.

Vinsanto: Santorini's Liquid Dessert

- After dinner, treat yourself to a glass of Vinsanto, Santorini's famous dessert wine. Made from sun-dried Assyrtiko grapes, this amber-colored nectar is rich with flavors of dried fruits, honey, and a subtle smokiness that echoes the island's volcanic past.

- Sip it slowly, savoring how the sweetness is balanced by a refreshing acidity. It's the perfect accompaniment to a plate of local cheeses or traditional Greek desserts like baklava. For a truly indulgent experience, drizzle a bit over some vanilla ice cream – it's a simple yet luxurious dessert that captures the essence of laid-back Santorinian evenings.

Vineyard Tours: Walking Through Living History

- To fully appreciate Santorini's wines, lace up your walking shoes and join a vineyard tour. As you stroll through the ancient vineyards, some with vines over 100 years old, you'll gain a deeper understanding of the island's unique viticulture.

- Pay attention to the volcanic soil beneath your feet – a mixture of pumice stone, volcanic ash, and lava fragments. This poor soil, combined with the lack of rainfall, forces the vines to dig deep for water and nutrients, resulting in grapes with intense flavors and high acidity.

- Many tours end with a tasting session at sunset. As you raise your glass, watching the sun dip into the Aegean, you'll understand why Santorini's wines are more than just a drink – they're a living connection to the island's history and terroir.

Cooking Classes and Food Tours: Hands-On Culinary Adventures

Mastering Santorinian Cuisine

- For those who want to take a piece of Santorini's culinary magic home with them, cooking classes are an absolute must. Imagine spending a morning in a sun-drenched kitchen, learning to craft those perfect tomatokeftedes or mastering the art of fava preparation.

- Many classes start with a visit to a local market or farm, where you'll learn to select the best ingredients. As you pick sun-warmed tomatoes off the vine or carefully choose the perfect white eggplant, you'll gain an appreciation for the quality of Santorini's produce.

- Back in the kitchen, under the guidance of a local chef, you'll discover the secrets behind Santorini's flavors. Learn how a pinch of wild thyme can elevate a dish, or how the judicious use of capers adds a burst of briny goodness. These are the little touches that transform good food into unforgettable meals.

- As you sit down to enjoy the fruits of your labor, paired with a glass of local wine, you'll feel a deep connection to the island's culinary heritage. And the best part? You'll take these skills home with you, able to recreate a taste of Santorini in your own kitchen.

Food Tours: A Moveable Feast

- For those who prefer to leave the cooking to the experts, food tours offer a delicious way to explore Santorini's culinary landscape. These guided experiences take you off the beaten path, introducing you to hidden gems and local favorites that you might otherwise miss.

- As you wind your way through narrow village streets, stopping at family-run tavernas and artisanal producers, you'll taste the true flavors of Santorini. Sample sun-dried tomatoes bursting with concentrated sweetness, or try your hand at making traditional phyllo pastry.

- Many tours include visits to local producers. You might find yourself in a small cheese-making facility, learning how the island's unique environment influences the flavor of the local goat cheese. Or perhaps you'll visit a tomato processing plant, discovering how those tiny, flavor-packed tomatoes are transformed into velvety pastes and sauces.

Best Restaurants and Tavernas: Where to Eat Like a Local

Selene: A Gastronomic Journey Through Time

- For a truly special dining experience, book a table at Selene. This Michelin-starred restaurant in Pyrgos village has been at the forefront of Santorinian cuisine for over 30 years. Here, traditional recipes are reimagined with modern techniques, creating dishes that are both familiar and excitingly new.

- As you dine on the terrace, overlooking the patchwork of vineyards below, you might be served a deconstructed moussaka or a playful take on traditional dolmades. Each dish is a celebration of local ingredients, presented with artistic flair. The wine list, curated by knowledgeable sommeliers, offers the perfect accompaniment to your meal, showcasing the best of Santorini's vintages alongside carefully selected Greek and international wines.

To Psaraki: Fresh Catches and Sea Views

- For the freshest seafood on the island, make your way to To Psaraki in Vlychada. This unassuming taverna, perched above the picturesque fishing harbor, serves up the catch of the day with simple, flavorful preparations that let the quality of the ingredients shine.

- Order the fish of the day, grilled to perfection and dressed with nothing more than a drizzle of local olive oil and a squeeze of lemon. Pair it with a crisp Assyrtiko and a Greek salad made with sweet, juicy Santorinian cherry tomatoes. As you dine, watch the fishing boats bob in the harbor below – tomorrow's catch making its way home.

Metaxy Mas: A Hidden Gem

Tucked away in the village of Exo Gonia, Metaxy Mas is a local favorite that's worth seeking out. This traditional taverna serves up generous portions of home-style Greek cooking in a cozy, unpretentious setting.

Don't miss their slow-cooked lamb kleftiko, tender meat that falls off the bone, infused with garlic and herbs. Their dakos – a Cretan-inspired dish of barley rusks topped with grated tomato, feta, and olive oil – is a perfect light meal or starter. The owners are known for their warm hospitality, often treating guests to a complimentary dessert or a shot of house-made raki at the end of the meal.

Chapter 6

Cultural Immersion and Historical Sites

The island's rich history and vibrant culture offer visitors a chance to step back in time and connect with ancient civilizations. From prehistoric ruins to Byzantine castles, Santorini's historical sites tell a fascinating story of human resilience and creativity.

Ancient Akrotiri: The Minoan Pompeii

Hidden beneath layers of volcanic ash for millennia, Ancient Akrotiri stands as a testament to the advanced Minoan civilization that once thrived on Santorini. This Bronze Age settlement, buried by a massive volcanic eruption around 1600 BCE, provides an unparalleled glimpse into daily life in the ancient Aegean world.

- As you walk through the excavated streets of Akrotiri, you will see well-preserved multi-story buildings, intricate drainage systems, and pottery workshops. The site's most striking feature is the remarkable frescoes that adorned the walls of wealthy homes. These colorful paintings depict scenes of daily life, religious rituals, and the natural world, offering insights into the beliefs and customs of the Minoan people.

- One particularly noteworthy fresco is the "Flotilla Fresco," which shows a fleet of ships sailing between two ports. This masterpiece not only showcases the artistic skills of the Minoans but also hints at their seafaring prowess and trading relationships with other Mediterranean cultures.

- To fully grasp the significance of Akrotiri, it's worth hiring a licensed guide. They can bring the ancient city to life, pointing out details you might otherwise miss and explaining the theories about the site's sudden abandonment. As you listen to their tales of ancient life, you might find yourself wondering about the fate of the city's inhabitants and the cataclysmic event that both destroyed and preserved their home.

Before leaving, stop by the on-site museum to see some of the artifacts uncovered during excavations. From everyday tools to elaborate jewelry, these objects offer a tangible connection to the people who once called Akrotiri home.

Museum of Prehistoric Thera

To complement your visit to Akrotiri, head to the Museum of Prehistoric Thera in Fira. This modern museum houses an impressive collection of artifacts from Akrotiri and other prehistoric sites on Santorini.

- The museum's exhibits are arranged chronologically, guiding you through the island's history from the Late Neolithic period (4th millennium BCE) to the Late Cycladic I period (17th century BCE). As you move through the galleries, you'll see how Santorini's inhabitants progressed from simple farming communities to sophisticated urban centers.

- One of the museum's highlights is the gold ibex figurine, a delicate sculpture that showcases the Minoans' extraordinary metalworking skills. Another must-see is the collection of ceramic vases, many of which still bear vibrant painted decorations despite their age.

- The museum also features several frescoes rescued from Akrotiri. These include the famous "Blue Monkeys" fresco, which depicts playful primates in an exotic landscape, hinting at the Minoans' far-reaching trade connections.

Before you leave, take a moment to study the detailed models of ancient Theran houses. These reconstructions, based on archaeological evidence, give you a clear picture of how the island's inhabitants lived before the catastrophic eruption.

Byzantine Castle Ruins

While Santorini is best known for its prehistoric remains, the island also boasts several medieval sites that are worth exploring. The Byzantine castle ruins scattered across the island offer a glimpse into Santorini's tumultuous history during the Middle Ages.

- Pyrgos, once the capital of Santorini, is home to one of the best-preserved castle settlements on the island. As you climb the winding paths to the top of the hill, you'll pass by white-washed houses and tiny churches, many of which date back to the 15th century.

- At the summit, you will find the ruins of Kasteli Castle. Built in the 13th century, this fortress once protected the island's inhabitants from pirate raids. Today, only portions of the outer walls remain, but the panoramic views from the top are breathtaking. On a clear day, you can see all the way to Oia in the north and Akrotiri in the south.

- Another notable castle ruin is Skaros Rock in Imerovigli. This imposing volcanic outcrop was once crowned by a formidable Venetian fortress. Although little remains of the castle itself, the hike to Skaros offers stunning views of the caldera and a chance to visit the tiny church of Theoskepasti, built into the side of the rock.

- For a less-visited but equally fascinating site, head to the ruins of Emporio Castle. This circular fortress, dating from the 15th century, encircles the village's highest point. As you wander through the narrow alleys within the castle walls, you'll come across several well-preserved churches adorned with beautiful frescoes.

Traditional Greek Festivals and Events

To truly understand Santorini's culture, try to time your visit with one of the island's traditional festivals. These events, deeply rooted in Greek Orthodox traditions, offer a window into local customs and beliefs.

- One of the most important celebrations is the Feast of the Assumption of the Virgin Mary on August 15th. This holiday is marked by religious processions, traditional music, and dancing in villages across the island. In Pyrgos, locals carry an icon of the Virgin Mary through the streets, while in Emporio, the festivities include a re-enactment of a traditional Santorinian wedding.

- If you're visiting in September, don't miss the Ifestia Festival. This event commemorates the volcanic eruptions that shaped Santorini, combining mythology with modern spectacle. The highlight is a impressive fireworks display over the caldera, designed to mimic a volcanic eruption.

- For a taste of Santorini's maritime heritage, check out the Fisherman's Feast in the coastal village of Vlychada. Held in June, this festival celebrates the island's fishing traditions with boat races, fresh seafood, and live music.

Wine lovers should plan their trip around the Vedema, or grape harvest, which typically takes place in late August or early September. Many wineries open their doors to visitors during this time, offering a chance to participate in traditional grape-stomping and enjoy freshly pressed wine.

Cultural Workshops and Classes

- For a hands-on approach to Santorini's culture, consider joining a workshop or class. Many local artisans offer sessions where you can learn traditional crafts and skills.

- Try your hand at pottery making in Megalochori, where you can learn the techniques used by Santorinian potters for generations. As you shape the local clay on a potter's wheel, you'll gain a new appreciation for the ceramic artifacts you've seen in the island's museums.

- For a taste of Santorini's culinary traditions, join a cooking class in Oia. Learn how to prepare classic dishes like tomato fritters and fava bean puree using local ingredients and time-honored techniques. Many classes include a visit to a local market or farm, where you'll learn about the island's unique agricultural practices.

- Photography enthusiasts can join workshops that focus on capturing Santorini's iconic landscapes and architecture. These sessions often include visits to off-the-beaten-path locations, allowing you to photograph aspects of the island that many tourists miss.

For a more spiritual experience, try a yoga or meditation class held in a traditional cave house or on a secluded beach. These sessions often incorporate elements of Greek philosophy and mythology, offering a unique blend of ancient wisdom and modern wellness practices.

Local Art Galleries and Studios

Santorini's dramatic landscapes and rich history have long inspired artists, and the island boasts a thriving contemporary art scene. Visiting local galleries and studios offers insight into how modern creators interpret Santorini's cultural heritage.

- In Oia, you'll find several galleries showcasing works by Greek and international artists. Many of these spaces are housed in traditional cave houses, creating a unique backdrop for the artwork. Look for pieces that incorporate local materials like volcanic sand or pumice stone, blending Santorini's natural elements with artistic expression.

- For a more intimate experience, seek out artists' studios in less touristy villages like Megalochori or Emporio. Many local painters and sculptors welcome visitors, offering a chance to see works in progress and discuss their creative process.

- Don't overlook Santorini's traditional crafts. In Pyrgos, you can visit workshops where artisans create intricate embroidery and lace, continuing techniques passed down through generations. In Oia, look for jewelry makers who incorporate local materials like volcanic glass into their designs.

Religious Sites and Traditions

While Santorini's ancient history is fascinating, the island's living religious traditions are equally compelling. The numerous blue-domed churches that dot the landscape are not just photogenic landmarks but active centers of worship and community life.

- Visit the Orthodox Metropolitan Cathedral in Fira, the island's largest church. Built in the 19th century, its ornate interior features beautiful frescoes and intricate woodcarvings. If possible, attend a service to experience Greek Orthodox rituals firsthand.

- For a more unusual religious site, seek out the Catholic Cathedral of St. John the Baptist in Fira. This pink-domed church, built in the 19th century, stands as a reminder of the Venetian influence on the island.

- One of Santorini's most unique religious structures is the Chapel of Panagia Theoskepasti in Imerovigli. Built into the side of Skaros Rock, this tiny church offers breathtaking views of the caldera. Local legend claims that the icon of the Virgin Mary housed in the church was found miraculously on the rock.

If you're interested in monastic life, visit the Monastery of Profitis Ilias, perched on Santorini's highest peak. Founded in 1711, the monastery played a crucial role in preserving Greek language and culture during Ottoman rule. Today, it houses a small museum of ecclesiastical artifacts and offers panoramic views of the entire island.

Chapter 7

Outdoor Activities and Natural Wonders

S antorini's outdoor offerings go far beyond its famous sunsets. The island's unique geography, shaped by volcanic activity, creates a playground for nature lovers and adventure seekers. From hiking trails with panoramic views to underwater explorations, Santorini's natural wonders await your discovery.

Hiking the Caldera Trail

The Caldera Trail, stretching from Fira to Oia, ranks as one of the most scenic hikes in the world. This 10-kilometer (6.2-mile) path hugs the edge of the caldera, offering unmatched views of the Aegean Sea and the volcanic islands at every turn.

- Starting in Fira, the trail winds through the villages of Firostefani and Imerovigli before reaching Oia. Along the way, you'll pass by blue-domed churches, traditional Cycladic houses, and luxury hotels carved into the cliffside.

- The hike typically takes 3-5 hours, depending on your pace and how often you stop for photos (which will be often). It's best to start early in the morning to avoid the midday heat. Wear sturdy shoes, bring plenty of water, and don't forget sunscreen and a hat.

- As you walk, keep an eye out for the diverse plant life that thrives in this harsh environment. You might spot phrygana, a low-growing shrub adapted to the dry conditions, or capers clinging to the rocky slopes.

- The trail offers several detours worth taking. In Imerovigli, a short side path leads to Skaros Rock, the ruins of a Venetian castle with panoramic views. Near Oia, you can descend to Armeni Bay, a picturesque port accessed by 300 steps.

- Upon reaching Oia, treat yourself to a well-deserved meal at one of the village's tavernas. As you relax with a cold drink, you'll have a new appreciation for Santorini's dramatic landscape and the forces that shaped it.

Exploring the Volcano and Hot Springs

No visit to Santorini is complete without a trip to Nea Kameni, the active volcanic island in the center of the caldera. Boat tours depart regularly from the old port of Fira, taking you across the caldera to this lunar-like landscape.

- As you approach Nea Kameni, you'll notice the stark contrast between its dark, rocky shores and Santorini's white cliffs. Stepping onto the island feels like walking on another planet. A guide will lead you along rocky paths to the crater, explaining the volcano's history and geology along the way.

- At the summit, peer into the crater and feel the heat rising from the ground. Sulfurous vents serve as reminders that the volcano is merely dormant, not extinct. The panoramic views from the top offer a unique perspective on Santorini and the surrounding islands.

- After exploring Nea Kameni, most tours stop at the nearby island of Palea Kameni for a swim in the hot springs. As you approach, you'll notice the sea changing color from deep blue to a rusty orange due to the mineral-rich waters.

- The boat will anchor offshore, allowing you to swim to the springs. The water here is warmer than the surrounding sea, heated by underground volcanic activity. Many believe these sulfur-rich waters have therapeutic properties, soothing skin conditions and aiding relaxation.

Note that the iron content in the water can stain light-colored swimwear, so it's best to wear darker colors. Also, the swim to the springs can be challenging for some, so assess your swimming abilities before taking the plunge.

Scuba Diving and Snorkeling

While Santorini's beaches might not match the soft sands of other Greek islands, its underwater world is truly spectacular. The volcanic activity that shaped the island has created unique underwater landscapes teeming with marine life.

- Several dive centers on the island offer courses and excursions for all skill levels. For beginners, the sheltered bay of Caldera Beach provides calm waters and good visibility to practice basic skills.

- More experienced divers should head to the Nea Kameni crater dive site. Here, you can explore underwater lava formations and swim through caves created by ancient lava flows. The clear waters allow for excellent visibility, often exceeding 30 meters (100 feet).

- The Wall dive site, located off the southern coast of Santorini, offers a dramatic underwater cliff face dropping to depths of over 200 meters (656 feet). This site often attracts larger pelagic fish and is a favorite among advanced divers.

- For those who prefer to stay closer to the surface, snorkeling provides an accessible way to explore Santorini's marine environment. The waters around Mesa Pigadia beach on the south coast offer good snorkeling opportunities, with rocky outcrops providing shelter for a variety of fish species.

- Many boat tours include snorkeling stops at secluded bays around the caldera. These trips often provide equipment and guidance, making them a good option for beginners or those traveling without their own gear.

Santorini's Unique Flora and Fauna

Despite its arid climate and volcanic soil, Santorini hosts a surprising diversity of plant and animal life. Many species have adapted to the harsh conditions, resulting in unique ecosystems found nowhere else in the world.

- The island's most famous agricultural product, the Santorini tomato, is a prime example of this adaptation. These small, sweet tomatoes thrive in the volcanic soil and require minimal water. You'll find them in many local dishes, particularly the popular tomato fritters.

- Another unique plant is the Santorini capers. These edible flower buds grow wild on the island, often seen clinging to stone walls or rocky outcrops. Their intense flavor is a staple in many traditional Santorinian recipes.

- For a comprehensive look at the island's plant life, visit the Botanical Garden of Santorini near Fira. This small but well-maintained garden showcases native species and explains their uses in traditional medicine and cuisine.

- Birdwatchers will find Santorini rewarding, especially during migration seasons. The caldera cliffs provide nesting sites for several seabird species, including the yellow-legged gull and Eleonora's falcon. The wetlands near Vlychada beach attract waders and waterfowl.

- In the waters around Santorini, you might spot dolphins playing in the wake of your boat. Monk seals, while rare, are occasionally seen along the less developed parts of the coastline.

- The island is also home to several endemic insect species, including the Santorini wall lizard, found nowhere else in the world. Keep an eye out for these small, agile creatures sunning themselves on rocks or old walls.

Sunset and Stargazing

Santorini's sunsets are world-famous for good reason, but the island's natural spectacles don't end when the sun dips below the horizon. The clear, dark skies over Santorini offer excellent conditions for stargazing.

- For the classic sunset experience, head to Oia. Arrive early to secure a good spot along the castle walls. As the sun sinks towards the horizon, watch how the changing light paints the white buildings in shades of pink and gold.

- For a less crowded sunset spot, try Prophet Elias Monastery, the highest point on the island. From here, you can watch the sun set behind the entire island, with the caldera spread out below you.

- After dark, the real show begins. Away from the village lights, the night sky comes alive with stars. The lack of light pollution, especially on the east coast of the island, allows for excellent stargazing conditions.

- For a guided astronomy experience, join a stargazing tour. These often include transportation to a dark sky location and the use of telescopes. Guides will point out constellations and share Greek myths associated with the stars.

- If you're visiting in August, try to catch the Perseid meteor shower. Find a dark beach or hilltop, lay back, and watch for shooting stars streaking across the sky.

Water Sports and Beach Activities

While Santorini isn't known for long, sandy beaches, its unique coastal areas offer plenty of opportunities for water sports and seaside fun.

- Perissa and Kamari, the island's black sand beaches, are popular spots for water sports. Here you can try jet skiing, parasailing, or paddleboarding. The consistent winds on these beaches also make them good for windsurfing, especially for beginners.

- For a more relaxed beach day, head to Red Beach near Akrotiri. The stunning red cliffs contrasting with the blue sea make this one of Santorini's most picturesque spots. The pebbly shore and crystal-clear waters are perfect for snorkeling.

- Vlychada Beach, with its wind-sculpted cliffs, offers a more secluded experience. The long stretch of dark sand provides plenty of space for sunbathing or beach walks. The nearby marina is a good spot to arrange sailing trips around the island.

- For a unique beach experience, visit White Beach, accessible only by boat or a challenging hike. The white cliffs and dark sand create a striking landscape, and the secluded location means it's often less crowded than other beaches.

Rock Climbing

- Santorini's volcanic cliffs provide exciting opportunities for rock climbing. While not as well-known as other climbing destinations in Greece, the island offers some unique routes with breathtaking views.

- The main climbing area is located near Kamari, where a series of bolted routes cater to various skill levels. The volcanic rock provides good grip but can be sharp, so gloves are recommended for beginners.

- For experienced climbers, the cliffs around the caldera offer more challenging routes. However, these are not bolted and require traditional climbing skills and equipment. Always check with local climbing guides or shops for current conditions and safety information before attempting these routes.

- Several companies on the island offer guided climbing experiences, providing equipment and instruction for all levels. These tours often combine climbing with hiking, offering a comprehensive outdoor adventure.

Horseback Riding

- Exploring Santorini on horseback provides a unique perspective on the island's landscape. Several stables offer riding experiences suitable for all levels, from beginner trail rides to beach gallops for experienced riders.

- A popular route takes you through the vineyards of Megalochori, where you can admire the traditional basket-trained vines unique to Santorini. As you ride, your guide will explain the island's winemaking traditions and how the volcanic soil influences the grapes.

- For a memorable experience, book a sunset ride along the black sand beaches of Vlychada or Eros. The sight of the sun setting over the Aegean while you ride along the shoreline is truly magical.

- Some stables also offer multi-day treks, allowing you to explore more remote parts of the island. These trips often include stops at local tavernas and wineries, combining outdoor adventure with cultural experiences.

Cycling and Mountain Biking

- While Santorini's hilly terrain can be challenging for cyclists, it also offers rewarding rides with spectacular views. Renting a bike or joining a guided tour is a great way to explore the island's less-visited areas.

- The inland route from Fira to Oia, passing through traditional villages like Finikia and Vourvoulos, offers a less crowded alternative to the popular hiking trail. This ride takes you past vineyards and old windmills, with plenty of opportunities to stop and enjoy the views.

- For mountain biking enthusiasts, the rocky trails around Prophet Elias mountain provide some thrilling descents. The area around Ancient Thera also offers good off-road riding, with the added bonus of passing by archaeological sites.

- Several companies on the island offer bike rentals and guided tours. E-bikes are also available, making it easier to tackle Santorini's hills and allowing you to cover more ground.

Kayaking and Stand-Up Paddleboarding

- Kayaking and stand-up paddleboarding (SUP) offer unique ways to explore Santorini's coastline from sea level. These activities allow you to access secluded coves and beaches not reachable by land.

- Guided kayak tours often depart from Akrotiri, taking you along the south coast of the island. You'll paddle past the White and Red beaches, with opportunities to stop for swimming and snorkeling. Some tours include a visit to the hot springs near Nea Kameni.

- Stand-up paddleboarding is popular at the calmer beaches like Kamari and Perissa. Early morning is the best time for SUP, when the water is often mirror-smooth and you can watch the sun rise over the Aegean.

- For a challenge, experienced paddlers can attempt to circumnavigate the small island of Thirasia, across the caldera from Santorini. This trip offers a different perspective on the main island and a chance to explore Thirasia's quiet beaches.

Chapter 8

Day Trips and Island Hopping

While Santorini offers plenty to keep visitors busy, venturing beyond its shores can add depth to your Greek island experience. The surrounding Cycladic islands each have their own unique character, offering new landscapes, flavors, and cultural experiences. Here's a guide to some of the best day trips and island-hopping options from Santorini.

Visiting Nearby Thirasia

- Thirasia, Santorini's quiet neighbor, sits just across the caldera. Often overlooked by tourists, this small island offers a glimpse of what Santorini might have been like before mass tourism.

- To reach Thirasia, catch a boat from Ammoudi Bay in Oia or the port of Ria. The journey takes about 10 minutes. Boats run regularly during the summer months, but schedules can be limited in the off-season, so check in advance.

- Upon arrival, you'll find yourself in the port of Korfos. From here, you can hike up to the main village of Manolas. The steep climb takes about 20 minutes but rewards you with panoramic views of Santorini across the caldera.

- Manolas feels like stepping back in time. The village's narrow streets are lined with traditional Cycladic houses, and you'll find few tourists. Stop at one of the local tavernas for a lunch of fresh seafood and locally grown produce.

- For beach lovers, head to Korfos Beach near the port. This pebbly beach offers clear waters perfect for swimming and snorkeling. You might have the entire beach to yourself, a rarity in the busy Cyclades.

- History buffs should make the trek to the monastery of Kimisis tis Theotokou. This 19th-century church sits at the highest point of Thirasia and offers stunning views of the entire caldera.

Before you leave, visit the cave houses in the village of Agrilia. These dwellings, carved into the volcanic rock, offer insight into traditional island life. Some are still inhabited today.

Thirasia is small enough to explore in a day, but if you want to fully embrace its slow pace of life, consider staying overnight. A handful of small guesthouses in Manolas offer simple but comfortable accommodations.

Excursions to Surrounding Cycladic Islands

Ios: The Party Island

- Just a short ferry ride from Santorini, Ios offers a different vibe. Known for its lively nightlife, Ios also boasts beautiful beaches and a picturesque main town.

- Catch an early morning ferry from Athinios port in Santorini. The journey takes about 40 minutes to an hour, depending on the type of ferry.

- Start your day in Chora, the main town of Ios. Its winding streets and white-washed buildings are typical of Cycladic architecture. Visit the Church of Panagia Gremiotissa for panoramic views of the island and sea.

- For beach time, head to Mylopotas. This long, sandy beach is one of the most popular on the island, offering clear waters and plenty of water sports options. For a quieter option, try Manganari Beach in the south of the island.

- History enthusiasts should visit the prehistoric settlement of Skarkos. This well-preserved site dates back to the Early Bronze Age and offers insight into ancient Cycladic civilization.

- As evening approaches, return to Chora. The town comes alive at night, with bars and clubs staying open until the early hours. Even if partying isn't your scene, the atmosphere is worth experiencing.

- The last ferry back to Santorini usually leaves in the early evening, so check the schedule carefully if you're planning a day trip.

Naxos: The Green Giant

- Naxos, the largest of the Cyclades, offers a diverse landscape of mountains, valleys, and long sandy beaches. It's a perfect day trip for those interested in history, outdoor activities, and local cuisine.

- The ferry ride from Santorini to Naxos takes about 1-2 hours, depending on the type of boat. Try to catch an early morning ferry to maximize your time on the island.

- Upon arrival, you'll dock in Naxos Town (Chora). Start your visit with a walk through the old town, climbing up to the Portara, a massive marble gate that's the remnant of an unfinished temple to Apollo.

- For beach time, head to Plaka Beach. This long stretch of golden sand is often considered one of the best beaches in Greece. The shallow waters make it perfect for families.

- If you're interested in history, visit the village of Apiranthos. Known as the "marble village" due to its marble-paved streets, Apiranthos is home to several small museums showcasing the island's archaeological and folkloric heritage.

- Naxos is famous for its agricultural products. Try the local graviera cheese, kitron liqueur, and potatoes, which are said to be the best in Greece due to the island's fertile soil.

- For a taste of traditional Naxian cuisine, head to one of the tavernas in the mountain village of Filoti. Here you can sample dishes made with local ingredients while enjoying views of the surrounding countryside.

- The last ferry back to Santorini usually departs in the early evening. If you find yourself enchanted by Naxos, consider extending your stay - many visitors find that a day isn't enough to fully explore this diverse island.

Paros: The Marble Island

- Paros, known for its fine white marble and traditional villages, offers a blend of history, beach life, and authentic Greek culture.

- The ferry ride from Santorini to Paros takes about 1-3 hours, depending on the type of ferry. Again, an early start will give you more time to explore.

- Begin your visit in Parikia, the island's main town and port. Wander through the old town, visiting the 4th-century

Panagia Ekatontapiliani church, also known as the Church of 100 Doors.

- For beach time, head to Golden Beach (Chryssi Akti) on the east coast. This long, sandy beach is popular for windsurfing due to the consistent Meltemi winds.

- Visit the picturesque fishing village of Naoussa in the north. Its small port, lined with tavernas and cafes, is one of the most photogenic spots in the Cyclades.

- If you're interested in the island's marble heritage, visit the abandoned marble quarries near the village of Marathi. These quarries supplied the marble for many famous ancient Greek sculptures.

- For a taste of local products, stop at one of Paros' many wineries. The island is known for its white wines made from the local Monemvasia grape.

- As with other day trips, be sure to check the ferry schedule for your return to Santorini. The last ferry usually departs in the early evening.

Boat Tours Around the Caldera

For those who want to stay closer to Santorini but still get out on the water, a boat tour around the caldera is a perfect option. These tours offer unique perspectives on Santorini's dramatic cliffs and the opportunity to swim in the caldera's clear waters.

Sunset Cruises

- Sunset cruises are among the most popular boat tours in Santorini. These typically depart from the old port of Fira or Ammoudi Bay in Oia in the late afternoon.

- As you sail around the caldera, you'll get close-up views of the island's multicolored cliffs. Many tours include a stop at the hot springs near Nea Kameni for a relaxing soak.

- The highlight of these cruises is watching the sun set over the Aegean. As the sky turns shades of pink and orange, you'll understand why Santorini's sunsets are world-famous.

- Most sunset cruises include dinner on board. You'll typically be served a selection of Greek dishes, often prepared with local ingredients. Some tours also include unlimited drinks.

- These cruises usually last 4-5 hours, returning after dark. It's a romantic way to end a day in Santorini and offers a different perspective on the island's famous sunsets.

Daytime Sailing Tours

- For those who prefer to be on the water during the day, several companies offer daytime sailing tours. These often include more swimming stops and the opportunity to snorkel in the caldera's clear waters.

- A typical daytime tour might include stops at Red Beach and White Beach, which are best accessed by boat. You'll have the chance to swim and snorkel in these picturesque coves.

- Many tours also visit the hot springs near Nea Kameni. The iron-rich waters here are said to have therapeutic properties, though be aware that they can stain light-colored swimwear.

- Lunch is usually included on these tours, often featuring a barbecue on board with fresh local ingredients.

Fishing Trips

- For a more active day on the water, consider joining a fishing trip. Several operators offer half-day or full-day fishing excursions in the waters around Santorini.

- These trips are suitable for both experienced anglers and beginners. The crew will provide all necessary equipment and instruction.

- You might catch species like grouper, sea bream, or even octopus. Many trips include the option to have your catch prepared for lunch on board.

- Fishing trips offer a chance to experience a traditional aspect of Greek island life and see Santorini from a different perspective.

Scuba Diving Excursions

- For certified divers, a day trip to some of Santorini's underwater sites can be a unique addition to your island-hopping experience.

- Several dive centers on the island offer boat trips to dive sites around the caldera. These might include the Nea Kameni crater, where you can explore underwater lava formations, or the Wall, a dramatic drop-off on the southern coast of the island.

- For those new to diving, many operators offer discover scuba experiences. These introductory courses allow you to try diving in a controlled environment, often in the sheltered waters of Caldera Beach.

Private Boat Rentals

- For those who prefer a more personalized experience, renting a private boat for the day is an option. This allows you to create your own itinerary, stopping wherever you like around the caldera.

- Several companies offer boat rentals, with or without a skipper. If you have the necessary qualifications, you can captain the boat yourself. Otherwise, hiring a local skipper is a good way to benefit from their knowledge of the area.

- A private rental allows you to avoid the crowds and set your own pace. You can linger at swimming spots, find secluded coves, or spend more time at the sites that interest you most.

This option is particularly good for small groups or families, offering a more intimate way to experience the waters around Santorini.

Practical Tips for Day Trips and Island Hopping

1. **Ferry Schedules:** Ferry schedules can vary significantly depending on the season. In summer, there are usually multiple daily connections to nearby islands. In the off-season, options may be more limited. Always check the most up-to-date schedules when planning your trip.

2. **Booking in Advance:** During peak season (July-August), it's advisable to book your ferry tickets in advance, especially for popular routes. You can usually do this online or through a local travel agency in Santorini.

3. Seasickness: The waters between the

Cycladic islands can sometimes be rough, especially when the Meltemi winds are blowing in summer. If you're prone to seasickness, consider taking preventative medication.

4. **Time Management:** Remember to allow plenty of time to get to and from the port in Santorini. The main port, Athinios, can get very busy, especially when multiple ferries are departing or arriving.

5. **Local Transportation:** When visiting other islands, check in advance what local transportation options are available. Some smaller islands have limited bus services or taxis, so you might need to rent a vehicle or book a tour to see the main sights.

6. Weather Considerations: Be aware that strong winds can sometimes cause ferry cancellations or delays. Have a backup plan in case your intended day trip isn't possible.

7. Pack Wisely: For day trips, pack essentials like sunscreen, a hat, water, and any medications you might need. If you're planning on visiting religious sites, remember to bring clothes that cover your shoulders and knees.

8. Respect Local Customs: Each island has its own character and customs. Be respectful of local traditions and dress codes, especially when

visiting churches or monasteries.

9. Environmental Awareness: The Cycladic islands are known for their natural beauty. Help preserve this by not littering, respecting wildlife, and following any local environmental guidelines.

Chapter 9

Practical Information and Tips

To make the most of your Santorini trip, it's crucial to have a good grasp of the practical aspects of visiting the island. This section covers essential information about transportation, money matters, health and safety, and sustainable tourism practices.

Transportation on the Island

Getting around Santorini efficiently is key to maximizing your time and enjoyment on the island.

Buses: The public bus system is the most economical way to travel around Santorini. Buses connect Fira, the main hub, to most villages and beaches. They're air-conditioned and generally reliable, but can get crowded during peak season. Schedules are posted at bus stations and online, but be prepared for potential delays during busy periods.

Taxis: Taxis are available but limited in number. You'll find taxi stands in Fira and at the airport, but it's often easier to have your hotel call one for you. Agree on the fare before starting your journey, as not all taxis use meters.

Car Rental: Renting a car gives you the freedom to explore at your own pace. Several local and international agencies offer rentals. Book in advance during high season. Remember, roads can be narrow and winding, and parking in popular areas like Oia can be challenging.

ATV and Scooter Rental: These are popular options for exploring the island. They're fun and can access areas larger vehicles can't, but exercise caution. Always wear a helmet and be aware that accidents involving tourists on ATVs and scooters are not uncommon.

Walking: In villages like Fira and Oia, walking is often the best way to get around. The streets are narrow and pedestrianized in many areas. Comfortable shoes are a must, as paths can be steep and uneven.

Cable Car: In Fira, a cable car connects the old port to the town. It's primarily used by cruise ship passengers but is open to all. The ride offers spectacular views of the caldera.

Donkeys: While donkey rides are still offered in some areas, particularly for the climb from the old port to Fira, many animal welfare organizations discourage this practice due to concerns about the animals' treatment.

Money Matters and Budgeting

Understanding the financial aspects of your trip can help you budget effectively and avoid surprises.

Currency: Greece uses the Euro. While credit cards are widely accepted in tourist areas, it's wise to carry some cash for smaller establishments or remote areas.

ATMs: You'll find ATMs in all major towns and tourist areas. Be aware that some may charge hefty fees for international withdrawals.

Tipping: Tipping isn't as ingrained in Greek culture as in some countries, but it's appreciated for good service. In restaurants, rounding up the bill or leaving 5-10% is common. For taxi drivers, rounding up to the nearest euro is typical.

Costs: Santorini can be expensive, especially in peak season and in popular areas like Oia. Budget accommodations and meals are available, but prices are generally higher than on many other Greek islands.

Tax Free Shopping: Non-EU residents can claim a VAT refund on certain purchases. Look for shops displaying the "Tax Free Shopping" sign and ask for a tax-free form with your purchase.

Bargaining: Unlike some other Mediterranean countries, bargaining isn't common in Greece outside of flea markets.

Health and Safety

Taking care of your health and staying safe will ensure a worry-free vacation.

Sun Protection: The Greek sun can be intense. Use high-SPF sunscreen, wear a hat, and stay hydrated, especially if you're out during the hottest part of the day.

Water: Tap water on Santorini is generally safe to drink but has a high mineral content that some find unpalatable. Many visitors prefer bottled water, which is widely available.

Healthcare: Santorini has a hospital in Fira and several medical centers. For EU citizens, the European Health Insurance Card (EHIC) provides access to state-provided healthcare. All visitors should have travel insurance that covers medical emergencies.

Pharmacies: These are well-stocked and can provide advice for minor ailments. Some medications that require prescriptions elsewhere may be available over the counter.

Safety: Santorini is generally very safe for tourists. However, take normal precautions against petty theft, especially in crowded areas.

Emergency Numbers:

- General Emergency: 112

- Police: 100

- Ambulance: 166

- Fire Department: 199

Sustainable Tourism Practices

As a popular destination, Santorini faces environmental challenges. Here's how you can help preserve the island's beauty:

Water Conservation: Santorini has limited freshwater resources. Take short showers, reuse towels, and be mindful of your water usage.

Plastic Reduction: Bring a reusable water bottle and shopping bag. Avoid single-use plastics where possible.

Respect Marine Life: Use reef-safe sunscreen when swimming. Don't touch or remove marine life while snorkeling or diving.

Stay on Paths: When hiking, stick to marked trails to prevent erosion and protect local flora.

Support Local: Choose locally-owned businesses and buy local products to support the island's economy.

Respect Local Culture: Dress modestly when visiting churches or monasteries. Ask permission before photographing locals.

Off-Peak Travel: Consider visiting during shoulder season to reduce strain on local resources during peak months.

Donkey Rides: If you choose to take a donkey ride, ensure the animals appear well-treated and not overburdened.

Waste Management: Always dispose of trash properly. Santorini has limited waste management facilities, so reducing your waste is crucial.

Seasonal Considerations

Santorini's character changes with the seasons. Here's what to expect:

High Season (June-August): This is the busiest and most expensive time. The weather is hot and dry, perfect for beach days. Book accommodations and activities well in advance.

Shoulder Season (April-May, September-October): These months offer pleasant weather and fewer crowds. It's an excellent time for outdoor activities like hiking.

Low Season (November-March): Many businesses close, and ferry services are reduced. However, you'll have a more authentic experience of local life. Be prepared for cooler, potentially rainy weather.

Practical Tips for Popular Activities

Sunset Viewing: The sunset in Oia is famously beautiful but extremely crowded. Arrive early to secure a good spot, or consider alternative locations like Skaros Rock in Imerovigli.

Wine Tasting: Many wineries offer tours and tastings. Book in advance, especially in high season. Consider a organized wine tour if you want to visit multiple wineries without worrying about driving.

Beach Visits: Not all of Santorini's beaches have facilities. Bring water, snacks, and sun protection. Some beaches, like Red Beach, require a short hike to access.

Hiking: The Fira to Oia hike is popular but challenging. Start early to avoid the heat, wear sturdy shoes, and bring water and snacks.

Boat Tours: If you're prone to seasickness, choose a larger boat for caldera tours. The waters can be choppy, especially in the afternoon when the wind picks up.

Archaeological Sites: Sites like Ancient Akrotiri can get hot. Visit early in the day and bring water. Guided tours can greatly enhance your understanding of these sites.

Shopping: For authentic local products, look for the "Authentic Santorini" label. Be cautious of mass-produced items sold as local crafts.

Photography: The light in Santorini is fantastic for photography, especially during the (golden hours) around sunrise and sunset. Respect "no photography" signs in churches and museums.

Communication and Connectivity

Staying connected in Santorini is generally easy, but here are some things to keep in mind:

WiFi: Most hotels, restaurants, and cafes offer free WiFi. Connection speeds can vary.

Mobile Data: If your home mobile plan doesn't cover Greece, consider buying a local SIM card for data access. These are available at the airport and in mobile phone shops in larger towns.

Post: The main post office is in Fira. Many hotels will also assist with mailing postcards or packages.

Booking and Reservations

Santorini is a popular destination, so planning ahead is crucial, especially in high season.

Accommodations: Book well in advance, especially for stays between June and September. The best hotels often fill up months ahead.

Restaurants: Popular restaurants, especially those with caldera views, can be booked solid in peak season. Make reservations for special meals.

Activities: Tours, particularly popular ones like sunset cruises, can fill up quickly. Book in advance to avoid disappointment.

Flights and Ferries: If you're island hopping, book your connections early. This is particularly important for flights, as seats can be limited.

Car Rentals: In high season, rental cars can be in short supply. Reserve yours well before your trip.

Local Events and Festivals

Check if your visit coincides with any local events or festivals. These can add a unique dimension to your trip but may also affect accommodation availability and prices.

Some notable events include:

- Easter celebrations (date varies, usually in April)

- Santorini Jazz Festival (usually in July)

- Ifestia Festival (around September 20th) - commemorates the volcanic eruptions with fireworks and events

- Megaron Gyzi Festival (August) - cultural events and concerts

Dealing with Crowds

Santorini can get very crowded, especially in peak season. Here are some strategies to help:

- Visit popular sites early in the morning or later in the evening

- Explore lesser-known villages like Pyrgos or Megalochori

- Consider staying in a quieter area like Imerovigli and visiting busy spots like Oia for shorter periods

- If you're on a cruise ship day trip, try to plan your activities for when most cruise passengers are back on board (usually late afternoon)

Chapter 10

Santorini for Special Occasions

Getaways and Honeymoons

For couples in love, Santorini is nothing short of paradise. The island's natural beauty and intimate atmosphere create the perfect backdrop for romance to flourish. Here are some ideas to make your romantic escape unforgettable:

1. Sunset Strolls in Oia: As the day winds down, take a hand-in-hand walk through the narrow, winding streets of Oia. Find a quiet spot along the caldera edge and witness the sun dip below the horizon, painting the sky in a mesmerizing array of oranges, pinks, and purples. It's a moment of pure magic you'll cherish forever.

2. Private Catamaran Cruise: Charter a catamaran for a day of sailing around the caldera. Sip champagne as you glide past hidden coves and dramatic cliffs. Many tours include stops for swimming and snorkeling in crystal-clear waters, followed by a romantic dinner on board as you watch the sunset.

3. Wine Tasting for Two: Santorini's volcanic soil produces unique, crisp wines. Visit a local winery like Santo Wines or Venetsanos Winery for a tasting session. Learn about the island's ancient winemaking traditions while savoring local varieties like Assyrtiko and Vinsanto.

4. Couples' Spa Day: Indulge in a pampering session at one of Santorini's luxury spas. Many high-end hotels offer couples' treatments using local ingredients like volcanic mud or grape extracts. Relax side-by-side with massages, followed by a soak in a private

jacuzzi overlooking the Aegean.

5. Candlelit Dinner in a Cave Restaurant: For a truly memorable meal, book a table at one of Santorini's cave restaurants. Places like La Cava in Oia or The White Cave in Imerovigli offer intimate settings carved into the cliffside, perfect for a romantic dinner.

6. Sunrise Hot Air Balloon Ride: For early risers, a hot air balloon ride at dawn offers a unique perspective of the island. Float gently over the caldera and surrounding villages as the first light of day bathes the landscape in a warm glow.

Honeymoon Tips:

- Book a hotel with a private balcony or terrace for intimate moments.

- Consider staying in less crowded villages like Imerovigli for more privacy.

- Let hotels and restaurants know you're on your honeymoon – many offer special perks or upgrades.

Destination Weddings

Santorini has become one of the world's most sought-after wedding destinations, and it's easy to see why. The island's dramatic landscapes and romantic atmosphere provide an unparalleled setting for saying (I do). Here's what you need to know about planning your Santorini wedding:

1. **Choosing Your Venue**: Santorini offers a variety of stunning locations for your ceremony and reception:

- Cliffside Terraces: Many luxury hotels have terraces overlooking the caldera, perfect for intimate ceremonies.

- Beach Weddings: For a more laid-back vibe, consider venues on Perivolos or Perissa beaches.

- Wineries: Combine your ceremony with wine tasting at picturesque locations like Pyrgos Restaurant or Venetsanos Winery.

- Traditional Churches: The blue-domed churches of Oia and Imerovigli make for iconic photo opportunities.

2. **Legal Requirements:** To legally marry in Greece, you'll need to provide several documents, including:

- Valid passports

- Birth certificates

- Certificate of No Impediment to Marriage

- Divorce or death certificates (if applicable)

It's advisable to work with a local wedding planner who can guide you through the process and help with translations.

3. **Best Time to Wed:** While Santorini is beautiful year-round, May to October offers the best weather for outdoor ceremonies. Keep in mind that July and August are peak tourist months, so venues and accommodations will be more expensive and crowded.

4. **Local Touches:** Incorporate Greek traditions into your celebration:

- Have a traditional Greek band play bouzouki music during your reception.

- Serve local delicacies like fava, tomatokeftedes, and Santorinian wine.

- Use olive branches or bougainvillea in your floral arrangements.

5. **Photography and Videography:** Santorini's unique landscape offers endless opportunities for stunning wedding photos. Schedule a pre-wedding photoshoot to capture the island's beauty without the time constraints of your wedding day.

6. **Guest Accommodations:** If you're having a destination wedding, consider booking a block of rooms at a few different hotels to accommodate various budgets. Provide guests with a list of activities and restaurants so they can make the most of their trip.

7. **Post-Wedding Activities:** Arrange group activities for your guests, such as a caldera boat tour or a guided walk through ancient Akrotiri, to thank them for making the journey.

Family-Friendly Activities

While Santorini is often associated with romance, it's also a fantastic destination for families. Here are some activities that will delight visitors of all ages:

1. **Beach Days:** The island's unique beaches offer fun for the whole family:

- Perissa and Perivolos: These long, black sand beaches have shallow waters perfect for young swimmers. They also offer water sports for older kids and teens.

- Monolithos: This quiet, family-friendly beach has a playground and basketball court.

- Red Beach: While swimming isn't always possible due to falling rocks, the dramatic red cliffs make for an exciting geological lesson.

2. **Ancient Akrotiri:** This archaeological site, often called the "Minoan Pompeii," brings history to life. Kids will be fascinated by the well-preserved frescoes and the story of how the ancient city was buried by a volcanic eruption.

3. **Santorini Water Park:** Located in Perissa, this small water park offers slides and pools that are perfect for cooling off on hot days.

4. **Donkey Rides:** While controversial due to animal welfare concerns, short donkey rides in Fira can be a memorable experience for children. Always choose reputable operators who treat their animals well.

5. **Open-Air Cinema:** Visit the charming open-air cinema in Kamari for family movie nights under the stars. They often screen family-friendly films in English with Greek subtitles.

6. **Cooking Classes:** Many local restaurants offer family cooking classes where kids can learn to make simple Greek dishes like tzatziki or Greek salad.

7. **Santorini Arts Factory**: This cultural center in Vlychada offers interactive exhibits and workshops that can be enjoyable for creative kids.

8. **Boat Tours:** Take a family-friendly boat tour around the caldera. Many tours include stops for swimming and snorkeling, as well as visits to the volcano and hot springs.

9. **Prophet Elias Monastery:** This hilltop monastery offers panoramic views of the entire island and a chance for kids to see traditional Greek Orthodox architecture.

10. **Ice Cream Adventures:** Make it a mission to try a different flavor of gelato each day from the many artisanal ice cream shops scattered across the island.

Family Travel Tips:

- Book accommodations with kitchen facilities to prepare meals and snacks for picky eaters.

- Consider renting a car for easier transportation around the island with kids in tow.

- Pack plenty of sunscreen, hats, and water bottles – the Santorini sun can be intense.

Solo Traveler's Guide

Santorini isn't just for couples and families – it's also an incredible destination for solo travelers. Here's how to make the most of your solo adventure on this stunning island:

Solo Travel Tips:

- Stay aware of your surroundings, especially at night, although Santorini is generally very safe.

- Don't be afraid to dine alone – many restaurants have bar seating perfect for solo diners.

- Consider renting a scooter or ATV for easy, independent exploration of the island.

Chapter 11

Seasonal Santorini: Year-Round Experiences

Each time of year brings its own magic to the island, offering visitors distinctly different experiences. From the vibrant energy of summer to the peaceful solitude of winter, Santorini transforms throughout the year, revealing new facets of its beauty and culture with each passing season.

Summer: Peak Season Highlights (June to August)

Summer in Santorini is a feast for the senses. The island pulsates with energy as tourists from around the world flock to its shores, eager to soak in the Mediterranean sun and immerse themselves in the quintessential Greek island experience.

1. Beach Life:

Summer is prime time for beach-goers. The island's unique beaches come alive with activity:

- Perissa and Kamari: These black sand beaches are perfect for sunbathing and water sports. The water is warm and inviting, ideal for long swims and snorkeling.

- Red Beach: While swimming might be restricted due to falling rocks, the dramatic red cliffs make for stunning photos.

- Vlychada: This lesser-known beach offers a more secluded experience with its moon-like landscapes.

Tip: Arrive early to secure a spot, especially on popular beaches like Perissa and Kamari.

2. Outdoor Dining:

Warm evenings are perfect for al fresco dining. Tavernas and restaurants set up tables outside, allowing you to enjoy local specialties under the stars. Don't miss the chance to try fresh grilled octopus or a traditional Greek salad while overlooking the caldera.

3. Sunset Cruises:

Summer evenings are ideal for boat trips around the caldera. Many tours offer sunset cruises with dinner included, providing a unique vantage point to watch the sun dip below the horizon.

4. Cultural Festivals:

Summer brings a variety of cultural events to Santorini:

- Megaron Gyzi Festival (August): Held in Fira, this festival features art exhibitions, musical performances, and theatrical shows.

- International Music Festival of Santorini (September): Classical music concerts in unique venues across the island.

5. Wine Tasting:

Visit local wineries like Santo Wines or Venetsanos Winery for tastings with a view. The warm weather makes it perfect to sip on chilled Assyrtiko while overlooking the vineyards.

6. Water Parks:

The Santorini Water Park in Perissa is a hit with families looking to cool off from the summer heat.

7. Nightlife:

Summer nights in Fira come alive with bars and clubs staying open until the early hours. The famous Koo Club and Enigma are popular spots for night owls.

Summer Tips:

- Book accommodations and restaurants well in advance, as this is the busiest season.

- Wear plenty of sunscreen and stay hydrated – the Santorini sun can be intense.

- Consider staying in less crowded villages like Imerovigli for a more relaxed experience.

Autumn: Grape Harvest and Wine Festivals (September to November)

As summer winds down, Santorini takes on a more relaxed pace. The crowds thin out, prices drop, and the island reveals a different side of its charm. Autumn is a favorite among many repeat visitors for its pleasant weather and unique experiences.

1. Grape Harvest:

September marks the beginning of the grape harvest. Many wineries open their doors to visitors, allowing them to participate in the grape-picking process:

- Estate Argyros: One of the oldest wineries on the island, offers harvest tours where you can learn about traditional winemaking methods.

- Gavalas Winery: A small, family-run winery that welcomes visitors to join in the harvest festivities.

2. Wine Festivals:

- Santorini Wine Festival (September): Held in Pyrgos, this festival celebrates the island's winemaking tradition with tastings, live music, and local food.

3. Hiking:

The cooler temperatures make autumn ideal for exploring Santorini's hiking trails:

- Fira to Oia Hike: This 10km trail offers stunning views of the caldera and passes through picturesque villages.

- Pyrgos to Ancient Thera: A challenging hike that rewards with panoramic views and historical sites.

4. Photography Opportunities:

The autumn light creates perfect conditions for photography. The softer sunlight enhances the colors of the landscape, making it a favorite season for photographers.

5. Local Life:

With fewer tourists, you'll have more opportunities to interact with locals and experience authentic island life. Visit local cafes in villages like Megalochori or Emporio to chat with residents.

6. Culinary Experiences:

Autumn brings a new menu of seasonal specialties:

- Fava: This yellow split pea puree is a Santorinian staple, perfect for cooler evenings.

- Tomatokeftedes: Tomato fritters made with the island's famous small, sweet tomatoes.

- Melitzanosalata: A smoky eggplant dip that's delicious with fresh bread.

7. Beach Tranquility:

While it might be too cool for swimming some days, the beaches are peaceful and perfect for long walks or picnics.

Autumn Tips:

- Pack layers – while days can be warm, evenings can get chilly.

- Some tourist facilities might start to close in late October, but most remain open through September and early October.

- Book a sunset sail to enjoy the changing colors of the sky without summer crowds.

Winter: Solitude and Local Life (December to February)

Winter in Santorini offers a completely different experience from the bustling summer months. While many tourist facilities close, the island doesn't shut down entirely. Instead, it offers a unique opportunity to experience the authentic, everyday life of Santorini.

1. Peaceful Exploration:

With few tourists around, you can explore popular sites like Oia and Fira without the crowds:

- Wander through the narrow streets and appreciate the architecture without bumping into other visitors.

- Visit the Museum of Prehistoric Thera or the Archaeological Museum of Thera and have the exhibits almost to yourself.

2. Winter Scenery:

While Santorini isn't typically associated with winter landscapes, the island takes on a different beauty:

- The white-washed buildings against gray skies create a striking contrast.

- On rare occasions, you might even see a dusting of snow on the highest points of the island, creating a surreal scene.

3. Local Traditions:

Winter is the time when many Greek holiday traditions come to life:

- Christmas in Santorini is a low-key affair, with beautifully lit boats (karavakia) displayed in town squares.

- New Year's celebrations often include the cutting of the Vasilopita, a traditional cake with a hidden coin for good luck.

- Epiphany (January 6th) is marked by the Blessing of the Waters ceremony in coastal villages.

4. Cozy Tavernas:

Many restaurants that remain open cater primarily to locals during this time:

- Enjoy hearty winter dishes like moussaka or stifado (beef stew) in the warmth of a traditional taverna.

- Strike up conversations with locals and learn about life on the island year-round.

5. Winter Activities:

While beach days are out, there are still plenty of things to do:

- Visit local workshops to see artisans at work, making everything from pottery to jewelry.

- Take cooking classes to learn traditional Greek winter recipes.

- Enjoy long lunches at seaside tavernas, watching the winter waves crash against the shore.

6. Hotel Deals:

If you don't mind that some facilities might be closed, you can find great deals on luxury accommodations during winter.

Winter Tips:

- Many hotels and restaurants close for the season, so check in advance and book accordingly.

- Ferry services are less frequent, so plan your arrivals and departures carefully.

- Bring warm clothing – while it rarely freezes, temperatures can drop, especially with the wind chill.

Spring: Wildflowers and Easter Celebrations (March to May)

As winter fades, Santorini bursts into life with the arrival of spring. This season offers a perfect balance of pleasant weather, fewer crowds, and the reawakening of the island's natural beauty.

1. Wildflower Blooms:

The landscape transforms with a carpet of wildflowers:

- Red poppies, yellow daisies, and purple thistles dot the countryside.
- Take a wildflower walk near Pyrgos or Emporio to see the island in full bloom.

2. Easter Celebrations:

Greek Orthodox Easter (usually in April or early May) is one of the most important holidays:

- Good Friday processions through villages are solemn and beautiful.
- Easter Sunday is marked by feasts and the cracking of red-dyed eggs.
- The village of Pyrgos is famous for its Easter celebrations, where thousands of tin cans with candles light up the hillside.

3. Outdoor Activities:

The mild weather is perfect for outdoor adventures:

- Hiking trails are at their most beautiful, with greenery and flowers along the paths.

- Bicycle tours around the island's less steep areas offer a unique perspective.

- Rock climbing in areas like Kamari is popular among adventure seekers.

4. **Agricultural Experiences:**

Spring is a time of agricultural activity:

- Visit small farms to see how locals cultivate Santorini's unique produce like white eggplants and cherry tomatoes.

- Some vineyards offer tours to see the unique "kouloura" method of vine training, where vines are woven into baskets to protect grapes from strong winds.

5. **Birdwatching:**

Spring migration brings various bird species to the island:

- Look for birds like the European bee-eater or the Eleonora's falcon.

- The wetlands near Vlychada beach are a good spot for birdwatching.

6. Reopening Festivities:

As tourist season approaches, many businesses reopen with special events:

- Art galleries in Oia often host opening exhibitions.

- New restaurants might offer special tasting menus to mark the start of the season.

7. Holy Week Activities:

The week leading up to Easter Sunday is filled with unique experiences:

- Attend a midnight Easter service at one of the island's beautiful churches.

- Join locals for the traditional lamb roast on Easter Sunday.

Spring Tips:

- Book accommodations in advance for Easter week, as it's a popular time for domestic tourism.

- Bring a light jacket and layers – while days can be warm, evenings might still be cool.

- Some tourist facilities might not be fully operational until May, so check in advance.

Year-Round Santorini:

While each season in Santorini has its unique charm, there are some experiences that can be enjoyed year-round:

1. Sunset Viewing:

No matter the season, Santorini's sunsets remain a breathtaking spectacle. Popular spots like the castle in Oia or Santo Winery offer stunning views year-round.

2. Wine Tasting:

Many wineries offer tastings throughout the year. Winter tastings might focus more on red varieties, while summer highlights crisp whites.

3. Hot Springs:

The volcanic hot springs near Palea Kameni are warm enough to enjoy even in cooler months.

4. Cultural Sites:

Museums and archaeological sites like Ancient Akrotiri are open year-round, although hours may be reduced in winter.

5. Culinary Experiences:

While menus may change with the seasons, Santorini's reputation for excellent cuisine holds true all year.

6. Photography:

Each season offers unique photographic opportunities, from summer's clear skies to winter's moody landscapes.

7. Village Exploration:

The charming villages of Santorini, with their winding streets and traditional architecture, are beautiful in any season.

Choosing when to visit Santorini depends on your preferences and what you hope to experience. Summer offers vibrant energy and bustling beaches, autumn brings wine harvests and pleasant hiking weather, winter provides a glimpse into local life and solitude, while spring bursts with natural beauty and cultural celebrations.

Conclusion

As you reach the end of your journey through this guide, it's clear that Santorini is more than just a picturesque destination; it's a vibrant tapestry woven from history, culture, and breathtaking landscapes. Every corner of this island invites exploration and sparks curiosity. Whether you've come for the stunning sunsets, the delicious cuisine, or the rich archaeological sites, Santorini offers a wealth of experiences that linger in your memory long after you leave.

The island's unique geography—formed by volcanic activity—provides a dramatic backdrop that enhances every moment. From the striking cliffs of Oia to the black sand beaches of Kamari, each location tells a story of nature's raw power and beauty. Walking through the narrow streets of Fira, you'll find charming boutiques, art galleries, and cafes where you can enjoy a leisurely cup of Greek coffee while watching the world go by. Each moment spent here is an invitation to appreciate the blend of tradition and modernity that defines this enchanting place.

The culinary scene in Santorini deserves special mention. The local cuisine is a celebration of fresh ingredients and age-old recipes. Dining in a seaside taverna while listening to the gentle waves is an experience that engages all the senses. Whether you're savoring a classic moussaka, indulging in fresh seafood, or trying the island's famous fava, every meal becomes a highlight of your trip. Pair your food with a glass of local wine, and you'll find that the flavors of Santorini add another layer to your understanding of the island.

History buffs will appreciate the rich tapestry of the island's past. From the ancient ruins of Akrotiri, where you can walk through remnants of a civilization preserved by volcanic ash, to the historical museums in Fira, each site reveals the story of a resilient culture. The island's history is not just something to learn about; it's woven into the very fabric of everyday life, seen in the architecture, the festivals, and the hospitality of the locals.

Speaking of the locals, one of the most delightful aspects of visiting Santorini is the warmth and friendliness of its inhabitants. They take pride in their island and are always willing to share stories, recommendations, or even a bit of their history. Engaging with them can turn a simple visit into a deeper experience, providing insights that guidebooks often overlook. Whether it's the fisherman at the port or the artisan in a workshop, every encounter has the potential to enrich your journey.

For those planning a trip, remember that Santorini is a year-round destination. Each season offers its unique charm, whether it's the vibrant blooms of spring, the sun-drenched beaches of summer, the colorful foliage of fall, or the serene quiet of winter. Choosing when to visit will depend on your preferences, but rest assured, Santorini has something to offer in every season.

In closing, your adventure in Santorini is just the beginning. The memories you create, the flavors you taste, and the sights you behold will stay with you long after you've returned home. This island has a way of etching itself into your heart, encouraging you to dream of your next visit. So, whether you've already booked your ticket or are just contemplating a trip, embrace the allure of Santorini. It's not just a destination; it's an experience that invites you to explore, savor, and appreciate the beauty of life.

So go ahead,embark on your own unique adventure. Safe travels, and may your journey be filled with unforgettable moments!

Made in the USA
Middletown, DE
20 March 2025

72990455R00079